Music
in the Romantic
Period

Music in the Romantic Period

An Anthology With Commentary

F. E. KIRBY

SCHIRMER BOOKS
A Division of Macmillan, Inc.

NEW YORK

Schirmer Books
A Division of Macmillan, Inc.
866 Third Avenue, New York, N. Y. 10022

Collier Macmillan Canada, Inc.

Library of Congress Catalog Card Number: 85-753047

Printed in the United States of America

printing number
1 2 3 4 5 6 7 8 9 10

Library of Congress Cataloging-in-Publication Data
Main entry under title:

Music in the romantic period.

1. Musical analysis—Music collections.   2. Music
appreciation—Music collections.   3. Music—19th century.
I. Kirby, F. E.
MT6.5.M89   1986   85-753047
ISBN 0-02-871330-3

Contents

Preface

The aim of this book is to provide an anthology of representative compositions of nineteenth-century Romantic music, with each selection accompanied by commentary, for use in courses in music history and theory. It thus forms a sequel to *Music in the Classic Period: An Anthology with Commentary* (1979). The intent, here as there, has been to emphasize complete works in their original scoring that are not found in other anthologies and that are readily available in recordings. The last criterion has not been difficult to meet: Indeed, only one selection (Grieg) appears not to have been recorded. With the other criteria the situation is different. For the Romantic period presents problems of selecting representative works that are much greater in number than did the Classic period. Since space has been a limiting factor, it has been much more difficult to select from a most varied repertory, in which compositions for orchestra, which frequently are not only long but also are scored for large ensembles, form a prominent part. Thus it has not always been possible to include complete works. Nor has it proved possible in all cases to avoid pieces that are included in other anthologies (e.g., the Liszt Concerto, the Brahms "Variations on a Theme of Haydn," and selections from Verdi and Mussorgsky, to name the most prominent). In all, the anthology comprises 58 separate items by 25 different composers. These include 6 complete major works, 22 short piano pieces, 11 songs, 5 complete movements or parts of larger instrumental works, and 14 numbers or excerpts from opera; three selections are fragments (Wagner, Mahler, and Strauss).

Central to this anthology has been the representation of the principal tradition of Romantic music, the art of instrumental music as developed in Germany and Austria, as will be explained in the Introduction. But space has been given to other traditions, notably Italian and French opera and the Nationalistic music of the late nineteenth century, so that a fuller view of the subject is conveyed. Even so, the individual instructor will want to supplement the compositions given here with others. To assist in this, an indication of what is offered in other anthologies is provided.

A few points: Translations of texts (songs and excerpts from operas), except for those that are underlaid, are by the editor. Such translations are literal, not poetic; the exception to this is the Wolf Glen scene from Weber's *Freischütz*. To save space, numbers are employed as follows: italicized Arabic numbers refer to the works of the same genre in a composer's output, such as Brahm's String Quintet *2*; lower-case Roman numbers are assigned to complete pieces that are part of a larger opus; for instance, Schumann's "Grillen" (op. 12 iv). Keys are indicated by italicized letters, capital for the major, lower-case for the minor. In bibliographical references, reprint editions are indicated by a slash and the letter *R*.

Unfortunately it has not been possible to take note of Leon Plantinga's recent and substantial *Romantic Music* and its companion anthology (New York: Norton, 1984).

For permission to reproduce material under copyright we are indebted to European American Music Distributors Corporation (Eulenburg Miniature Scores),

ix

C. F. Peters, Polygram, and William Mann and the Kunsthalle in Hamburg (West Germany). The Introduction has appeared in somewhat different form in the *Piano Quarterly*, No. 129 (33rd Year, Spring, 1985). Thanks go to two colleagues at Lake Forest College, Ann D. Bowen of the Department of Music and Arthur Miller, the College Librarian, for assistance of various kinds and for enabling the use of materials in the college's collections, as well as to Ellen Pearl of Highland Park (Illinois), who gave an early version of the text a close reading. Maribeth Anderson Payne and Kent Baird of Schirmer Books deserve much credit for whatever merit may be found in the commentaries. Finally, thanks go to two libraries where much of the work was done: Northwestern University and the State University of New York at Albany.

F.E.K.
Lake Forest College
May 1985

Abbreviations for Publications Frequently Cited

AMA   *Anthology for Musical Analysis*, ed. C. Burkhart, 3rd ed. (Englewood Cliffs, N.J.: Prentice-Hall, 1979)

C   *The Concerto, 1800–1900*, ed. P. Lang (New York: Norton, 1969)

CSM   *The Comprehensive Study of Music. Anthology of Music, II: From Beethoven through Wagner*, ed. W. Brandt et al. (New York: Harper, 1977)

MA 18-9   *Music and Aesthetics in the 18th and Early 19th Centuries*, ed. P. Le Huray & J. Day (Cambridge, England: Cambridge University Press, 1981)

MCP   *Music in the Classic Period: An Anthology with Commentary*, ed. F. E. Kirby (New York: Schirmer, 1979)

MO   *Music in Opera: A Historical Anthology*, ed. E. Brody (Englewood Cliffs, N.J.: Prentice-Hall, 1970)

MQ   *Musical Quarterly*

MR   *Music Review*

MSO   *Music Scores Omnibus, Part 2: Romantic and Impressionistic Music*, ed. W. Starr & G. Devine (Englewood Cliffs, N.J.: Prentice-Hall, 1958)

MWW   *Music in the Western World: A History in Documents*, ed. P. Weiss & R. Taruskin (New York: Schirmer, 1984)

NAWM   *Norton Anthology of Western Music, ii, Classic, Romantic, Modern*, ed. C. Palisca (New York: Norton, 1981)

NCS   *Norton Critical Scores* (New York: Norton, since 1967)

NSe   *The Norton Scores*, ed. R. Kamien, ii, 4th ed., expanded (New York: Norton, 1984)

PQ   *Piano Quarterly*

S   *The Symphony, 1800–1900*, ed. P. Lang (New York: Norton, 1969) .

SRMH   *Source Readings in Music History*, ed. O. Strunk (New York: Norton, 1950; also available separately).

Music in the Romantic Period

Introduction

Art that is based on expression, individuality, subjectivity, emotionality, and inspiration or enthusiasm (the last two terms originally had the same meaning) has come to be called *romantic*. The term is used in opposition to *classic*, art based on universality, balance, repose, reflection, and moderation. The term *romantic* comes from *romance*, related to medieval legends and epics. In the later eighteenth century it was applied to varieties of art that departed from Classical norms. In 1808–1809 the critic August Wilhelm Schlegel used *classical* for the literature of antiquity and *romantic* for European literature since the Middle Ages. Shortly thereafter, however, the term *romantic* came to be used in a general way for all that was perceived as new in literature, art, and music.[1]

A number of different characteristics apart from subjectivism and emotionality and those previously mentioned have been included under Romanticism: the portrayal of strange events and fantastic characters in settings remote in time and place (the Middle Ages, for instance), the prominence of the folk-like and naive, the nocturnal, the supernatural, and death. All of these elements can be found in the musical works of the nineteenth century. Yet an individual artwork does not have to contain all of them in order to qualify as romantic. The point of consistency was the avoidance of classical subjects and models.

The central idea clearly was that the artworks should be the personal—subjective—expression of the artists, themselves. Two aspects of the rationalistic classical aesthetics that prevailed in the first half of the eighteenth century are important here. First, the artwork should manifest Aristotle's idea of *mimesis*, should imitate nature. In music the imitation of nature had long been understood as referring to the imitation of human passions. This was particularly evident in the late Baroque, where the representation of human passions in music was carried out along entirely rationalistic lines, with standardized ways of representing various emotional states, as exemplified in what is known as the theory of affections. Second, the artwork was expected to conform to accepted standards of taste, such as Winckelmann's qualification of Greek art as "noble simplicity and quiet grandeur." Here too the dictates of reason were primary. The way to the Romanticism that gradually asserted itself throughout the eighteenth century involves on the one hand greater emphasis on the role of imagination, rather than reason, in the artwork, and on the other the acceptance of models that depart from Classical aesthetics as formulated, for instance, by Winckelmann: Gothic architecture and Shakespeare, that is to say, replace the Parthenon and Racine.

---

[1] See generally M. Abrams, *The Mirror and the Lamp* (New York: Oxford, 1953); L. Furst (ed.), *European Romanticism; Self-definition* (London and New York: Methuen, 1980); R. Wellek, "The Concept of Romanticism in Literary Criticism," *Concepts of Criticism* (New Haven: Yale, 1963), 128 ff. (esp. 134–7). See also MA 18-9 and SRMH.

1

While the notion that the artwork should be expressive of human feelings is very old—it goes back to antiquity and was revived as a central article in the aesthetics of the Renaissance—the other idea that such an expression should be individual and subjective—a confession, as it were, of the artists themselves (as Goethe once said, "all my works are fragments of a great confession"[2])—became important only in the eighteenth century. From this the extension to include spontaneity and inspiration or enthusiasm was entirely consistent. Here too the contrast with the older ideal of the artwork based on rational principles could hardly be more complete. The main idea was voiced by many writers in England, France, and Germany: Wordsworth and Victor Hugo emphasized the importance of feelings in poetry; Wordsworth and Coleridge laid stress on the primacy of imagination; the German poet Hölderlin put the matter succinctly: "man is a god when he feels, a beggar when he thinks."[3]

An underpinning to all this may be found in the philosophy of the time. Kant, proceeding from Hume's skepticism concerning the power of reason, defined the limits of what reason can accomplish. He thus implied a realm beyond reason, which in turn was seized upon by the Romantics, with their emphasis on subjectivity, intuition, and feeling. The creative artist came to be the artistic genius: As Kant put it, "genius is the talent that gives art its rules."[4]

Yet the terms *classic* and *romantic* are also used in a nonhistorical sense to denote basic types of artistic expression: the former for one that respects tradition and embodies reason, balance, and order, and the latter for one that emphasizes individuality and expression. The scholar Curt Sachs has referred to the two as *ethos* and *pathos* respectively.[5] Since both occur in the art of all historical periods, the additional use of the terms *classic* and *romantic* to designate the historical periods between 1750 and 1900, however one may divide them up, has made the situation more complex.

Most of the difficulties, however, are associated with the term *classic*. It is generally agreed that the great change in musical style took place around the middle of the eighteenth century, when the Italian Baroque repertory, which centered around the *opera seria*, gave way to a new art of instrumental music in the hands of German-speaking composers. This new art, which achieved an extraordinary perfection beginning in the 1770s and 1780s in the instrumental compositions of Haydn and Mozart and later in those of Beethoven and Schubert, has been referred to in the field of music history as *classic*. Yet this Classic period, the termination of which is by no means clear, is much more restricted than other epochs in the history of the art—it is not only short (30–80 years, depending on one's interpretation), but also localized, since its chief exponents lived and worked in Vienna. This use is doubtless due in part to the interest of German scholars in finding composers comparable to the great

---

[2] Goethe, *Dichtung und Wahrheit*, II, 7; see his *Werke* (Hamburger Ausgabe), ix (Hamburg: Wegner, 1955), 283.

[3] Hölderlin, *Hyperion*, in Book I; see his *Werke und Briefe*, i (Frankfurt: Insel, 1969), 298; see also readings in Furst, *European Romanticism*, and the quotations from Schumann in *MWW*.

[4] Kant, *Kritik der Urteilskraft*, No. 46; see the English ed., trans. J. Barnard (New York: Hafner, 1951), 150.

[5] Sachs, *The Commonwealth of Art* (New York: Norton, 1946), 199 ff.

group of Classical writers (Goethe, Schiller, Herder), who were also localized, in Weimar. The term has continued to be used in connection with these composers.

In one important sense the term *classic* retains its validity as the name for the later eighteenth and early nineteenth centuries in the history of music: *classic* in the sense of providing a model worthy of imitation. The principles and forms of the art of instrumental music established by the Viennese Classic composers undeniably provided the models for much nineteenth-century music. This is particularly true of Beethoven, four of whose symphonies (3, 5, 6, and 9) had a profound, indeed almost traumatic, effect on subsequent composers, as can be seen in various ways in the work of Schumann, Liszt, Wagner, and Bruckner, to name only the most important.

Of overriding importance for Romantic music was a new way of understanding the artwork. This took the form of a new twist given the old doctrine of *mimesis* (discussed earlier), which is known as the organic or vegetable theory of artistic expression. It holds that an artwork embodies the same principles and, particularly, processes, that are found in the natural world. By the end of the eighteenth century we find a new vitalistic conception of the artwork in general. An early example appears in Edward Young's influential *Conjectures on Original Composition*, where an artwork produced by an original genius is compared to a vegetable in the sense that it "rises spontaneously" and "grows, is not made."[6] Many others, particularly in Germany, took up the idea. It was dominant in Goethe, who referred specifically to the *spiritual-organic (geistig-organisch)* quality that artists must impart to their work; while A. W. Schlegel, whose ideas influenced Mme. de Staël in France and Coleridge in England, said that "[art,] like nature, should be autonomously creating, organized and organizing, forming living works, which move, not by an extraneous mechanism, like the pendulum on a clock, but by a force that lives within, like the solar system . . ."[7]

This idea has considerable applicability to music, as can readily be seen. The Baroque conception of singleness of affect, of expressive character, within a musical composition had been replaced around the middle of the eighteenth century by a multiplicity of contrast and variety. Symbolic of this change is not only the rise of the sonata principle itself in the eighteenth century, with its prominence of thematic development and variety of affect, but also the new interest in dynamics as an important element in musical composition. For this the exploitation of crescendo is a vital sign. This new attitude made possible the radically new and different music that developed in the late eighteenth century and continued with extensions and developments in the nineteenth. That is to say, it became possible for music to manifest directly and powerfully the experience of life: expectations, fulfillments, tensions, releases, intensifications, culminations, relaxations, and the like. Music thus became, as it were, a copy of basic life processes. Schiller expressed this well: "the whole effect of music . . . [is] the inner moving of the spirit through analogous externals to accompany and to illustrate."[8] Music's effects, that is to say, result from

---

[6] Young, *Conjectures on Original Composition* (London: Millar, 1759), 12; there are several modern editions.

[7] Goethe, "Einleitung in die Propyläen," *Werke* (Hamburger Ausgabe), xii (1953), 42; A. W. Schlegel, "Vorlesungen über schöne Literatur und Kunst," *Kritische Schriften*, ii (Stuttgart: Kohlhammer, 1963), 91; see also Furst, *European Romanticism*, 87-8.

[8] Schiller, "Über Matthisons Gedichte," *Werke* (Nationalausgabe), xxii (Weimar: Böhlau, 1958), 272.

the correspondences between its motions in time and those of our affects, our feelings. We are literally moved by the music, as the French *émouer* (English *emotion*) clearly signifies. Consistent with this is the frequent Romantic characterization of art as representing becoming, not being: *Werden*, not *Sein*.

While this applies to all music, it had particular relevance for instrumental music, which in the past had been considered devoid of intellectual content and thus had been accorded only secondary importance. This is reflected, for instance, in Kant. But now, with the new and powerful capacities attributed to the art, it became the principal kind of music. This idea is prominent in the writings of the early German Romantics. As E. T. A. Hoffmann put it: "When one speaks of music as an independent art, then what is meant should be instrumental music, which in disdaining any admixture with another art speaks purely the peculiar essence of the art that can only be recognized in it."[9]

This new art of instrumental music furthermore came to be regarded as one of sufficient scope and complexity to be compared with philosophy. According to Friedrich Schlegel "all music must be philosophical and instrumental."[10] Others felt music had a transcendent power to make the infinite manifest and to reveal the eternal, so that music took on mystical aspects. The very wordlessness of instrumental music, far from being a drawback, made possible the expression of things considered more profound than what was possible in any other form of art. Music thus came to be regarded as a kind of language in which it was possible to speak the unspeakable.

A new importance came to be attributed to music—specifically instrumental music—as compared with the other arts. This emerges clearly in two documents of early German Romantic literature, the *Herzensergiessungen eines kunstliebenden Klosterbruders* (*Outpourings from the Heart of an Art-loving Monastery Brother*) and the *Phantasien über die Kunst* (*Fantasies about Art*) by Wilhelm Heinrich Wackenroder and Ludwig Tieck, published in 1797 and 1799 respectively. We find here enthusiastic appreciations of art in general and music in particular. "No other art," they said of music, "can combine in such an unfathomable way the qualities of profundity, of power over the senses and dark, fantastic meaning."[11] They went so far as to claim that "music is certainly the last secret of belief, the mystic, the holy religion,"[12] thus elevating the art to a level comparable to religion.

This increase in the status of music relative to the other arts can also be found in German philosophical writings of the time. While both Kant and Hegel ranked poetry the highest among the arts, they both noted the special power of music. Kant regarded it as deficient in providing material for reflective thought, but he was also aware of its intense effect, greater than the other arts; Hegel considered music the most emotional art, since in it there was no separation between subject and object. In Schopenhauer's

---

[9] Hoffmann, *Schriften zu Musik* (Munich: Winkler, 1963), 34, trans. F. E. K. For another translation, see SRMH, 775.

[10] F. Schlegel, *Charakteristiken und Kritiken I* (Kritische Friedrich Schlegel-Ausgabe, ed. E. Eichner, 1, ii; Munich: Schöningh, 1967), 254.

[11] Wackenroder and Tieck, "Das eigentümliche innere Wesen der Tonkunst," *Phantasien über die Kunst* (Stuttgart: Reclam, 1973), 78; see, similarly, readings in MA 18–9 and SRMH.

[12] Wackenroder and Tieck, "Symphonien," *Phantasien über die Kunst*, 107. The attribution of specific passages to either Wackenroder or Tieck is a matter of controversy.

classification, however, music appears as the supreme art.[13] Moreover, there came an awareness in the thought of the time that the principles of music were fundamentally the same as those of the other arts, that all the arts were at bottom manifestations of the same thing. Novalis wrote in his *Fragmente*: "painting, plastic art . . . are but the figuring [*Figuristik*] of music." In the same spirit is the statement that architecture is frozen music, variously made by Goethe, Friedrich Schlegel, Schelling, and others. Later in the century Walter Pater came up with his famous phrase about "art approaching the condition of music."[14]

With all this comes the idea of *absolute music*: the new capacities attributed to the art of music gave rise to the idea that an instrumental composition could be autonomous, complete in itself, free (absolved) from any words or reference, content, and meaning, existing purely in, of, and for itself. The term, apparently first used by Wagner in 1846, is most commonly employed, then as now, in opposition to *program music*, where clear and frequently detailed extramusical meanings are expressed in a composition. But *absolute music* has also been used to suggest that music, by virtue of the power and range of its expressive capacities, can reveal the absolute. This is implicit in the passages from Schlegel and Tieck that have already been quoted.[15]

It is interesting parenthetically to reflect on the general historical context in which this new orientation in music developed. The late eighteenth century had witnessed two epochal revolutions, the American and the French, the latter leading directly into the turbulent time of Napoleon. Thereafter in Western Europe there took place a strong reaction, an attempt to reestablish in some sense things as they had been. But revolutionary movements continued. The nineteenth century also saw the establishment of Italy and Germany as nations. Musicians were necessarily affected by these events, in two famous cases directly involved: Wagner at the unsuccessful uprising in Dresden in 1848 and Verdi in the *risorgimento* ("resurgence," the movement to unify Italy). While Wagner was forced into exile for almost two decades, Verdi's efforts gained him a seat in the Italian parliament, which he held for a short time.

The nineteenth century was also an age of scientific and intellectual discovery and technological advances that totally transformed life. A few achievements may be given here as indications: Fulton and the steamship (1807); the first railroad, in England (1825); Faraday and the electric motor and generator (1831); the telegraph (1837); Daguerre and photography (1838); the first incandescent light bulb (1858); Darwin and the theory of evolution (1859); Edison and the phonograph (1878); Daimler and the internal-combustion engine (1889); Pavlov and the conditioned reflex (1905). An important consequence of much of this was the industrial revolution. Kenneth Clark

[13] Kant, *Kritik der Urteilskraft* (1790), No. 51–3; see trans. by Barnard (note 4), 164 ff. and also MA *18–9*; Hegel, *Ästhetik*, i (Frankfurt: Europaische Verlagsanstalt, 1966), 88–95; Schopenhauer, *Die Welt als Wille und Vorstellung* (1818), No. 50–2; see English ed., *The World as Will and Representation*, trans. E. Payne, i (Indian Hills, Colo.: Falcon's Wing Press, 1958), 237 ff. and also MA *18–9*; Hegel's lectures, held in the 1820s, were published posthumously.

[14] Novalis, "Fragmente," *Schriften*, ed. R. Samuel et al., iii (Stuttgart: Kohlhammer, 1960), 309; see also Abrams, *Mirror and Lamp*, 94 and 353 (n. 84), and also W. Pater, "The School of Giorgione," *The Renaissance* (New York: Mentor, 1973), 95.

[15] See esp. C. Dahlhaus, *Die Idee der absoluten Musik* (Kassel: Bärenreiter and Munich: Deutscher Taschenbuchverlag, 1978).

has referred to the age generally as that of "heroic materialism."[16] How all this accords with the notion of art as personal and subjective expression is an important question for the history of ideas, which can only be raised here.

Historically, the change in music that characterizes Romanticism started around 1820: a distinct shift in the repertory, as genres associated with the Romantic aesthetic came into prominence. Under the influence of new ideas concerning the expressive power of music, those genres of composition in which the link to literature or other arts was explicit not only grew in importance but over time came to displace the older, large forms of instrumental music. The new genres were for the most part small—the art song and character piece for piano are the most prominent—and characterized by lyricism. The emphasis went to melody as melodiousness took on a value in and of itself, rather than by virtue of its role in the larger context of the work. This attitude affected the sonata principle, the center of the old classic art, as melodious, lyric, themes replaced those characterized rather by generalized motivic components. Closely associated with this went a new emphasis on sound—sonority, tone, and color, as has been eloquently set forth by Einstein.[17] Instrumental music had replaced vocal music as the most respected kind of music, and now there was recourse to music in which its most basic manifestation—sound—appeared in individual, indeed unprecedented, ways. Composers sought specific colors produced by employing specific harmonies and textures, in specific registers, all to produce evocative, at times mysterious, and even magical effects.

None of this, of course, was entirely new; it all had appeared in the work of Haydn, Mozart, and Beethoven, to name only the most prominent. What is new is the matter of degree. In the Romantic music this new orientation based on melody and sound and associated with literary expression clearly became dominant. Even so there was a good deal of continuity between Romantic music and that of the late eighteenth century.

Therefore, to return to our earlier line of argument, it would seem suitable to speak of two central traditions in music between 1750 and 1900, each with its own emphasis, based to a large extent on repertory: a *classic tradition*, established first, in which the large forms of instrumental music formed the center; and a *romantic tradition*, in which compositions most often were conceived in relation to extramusical associations, usually literary, and in which the smaller lyric forms became prominent. Both traditions retained their validity throughout the nineteenth century. While some composers clearly were more involved with one than the other, in most cases the two stand side by side in a composer's work. Wagner's achievement, for instance, can be viewed in these terms, since it explicitly resulted from the application of thematic development (instrumental music) to a musico-dramatic work (vocal music) and was referred by Wagner himself specifically to Beethoven.

These two traditions were well recognized at the time. For example, Richard Strauss at the end of the century gave testimony to this perception of the situation in an acute if somewhat ungrammatical way:

---

[16] K. Clark, *Civilisation* (New York: Harper and Row, 1970).
[17] A. Einstein, *Music in the Romantic Era* (New York: Norton, 1947), 32.

The representatives of present-day music do divide themselves into two groups, the one for whom music is *expression* and which they treat as a language just as precise as a language of words. The others, to whom music is *sounding form*, that is, they assume for the work being composed some sort of general basic mood and develop the themes elicited from this according to a completely external musical logic.[18]

The new genres of the progressive Romantic tradition demanded new approaches to the art of composition. Liszt explained his principles for the composition of symphonic poems in his important essay on Berlioz, written in 1855:

In the so-called classical music the return and development of themes is determined by formal rules which are regarded as inviolable . . . In program music, in contrast, the return, change, variation and modulation of the motives is conditioned by their relation to a poetic idea. . . . All exclusively musical aspects, even though none are by any means left out of consideration, are subordinated to the treatment of the subject-idea. Thus the treatment and subject-matter in this type of symphony can claim an interest above the technical handling of the musical materials.[19]

Hand in hand with this goes a shift in the status of the musician and specifically the composer. Essentially this represented the continuation of a process started in the eighteenth century whereby composers formerly dependent on the old patronage system—that is, in the employ of a court or religious institution—became free artists, who sought their livelihoods by giving concerts, receiving commissions, honoraria from publications, fees from giving lessons, writing of criticism, and so on. This development, of course, is bound up with the rise of the middle class and the decline of the aristocracy. The consequences were enormous: the establishment of institutions for the teaching of music (conservatories), the proliferation of music-publishing houses and journals devoted to music, and the establishment later in the century of standing orchestras, among others—all of which have characterized musical life in the West down to our time.

The coupling of these developments with typically Romantic notions of music as the most expressive of the arts and of artists as special, set off from ordinary people by virtue of their talent, creates the background for one of the most characteristic features of musical life at the time: the virtuoso, gifted with extraordinary ability to play an instrument or to sing. Again, while the virtuoso performer had long been a feature of musical life, in the nineteenth century he or she assumed a position of peculiar importance. One such artist was the Italian violinist Niccolò Paganini, whose skill in playing seemed to border on the supernatural, an impression supported by his very appearance, the sunken cheeks (from an operation on his jawbone and the removal of his teeth), black hair, and brilliantly flashing eyes; moreover, he dressed in black.[20] Once Liszt, the great pianist, took over important aspects of what Paganini did, the

---

[18] Letter to the composer Bella, quoted by E. Krause, *Richard Strauss. Gestalt und Werk* (Leipzig: Breitkopf & Härtel, 1970), 221, trans. F. E. K.; see also English ed., *Richard Strauss. The Man and his Work* (Boston: Crescendo, 1969), 217. The expression "sounding form" ("tönende Form") is related to the famous and influential formulation of Hanslick ("tönend bewegte Formen").

[19] Liszt, *Gesammelte Schriften* v (Leipzig: Breitkopf & Härtel, 1882), 191, trans. F. E. K.; another translation is in *MWW*, 383.

[20] Contemporary description is in *MWW*, No. 98.

Romantic image of the virtuoso was born, an image that has retained its validity to the present day. Naturally, music in which the bravura element of virtuoso display is prominent became important in the repertory.

Thus the most basic features of *musical Romanticism* have been identified and described. Clearly far more than the notion of the artwork as the personal emotional expression of the artist themselves is involved. Two aspects appear crucial: first, the new vitalistic-organic conception of the musical artwork, by means of which instrumental music became preeminent among the different kinds of music and music itself rose in standing vis-à-vis the other arts. Second is the literary connection, as it were, where the composer not only frequently engaged in writing and editing, but also based compositions upon works of literature. Then, of course, there is the interest in sonority in and of itself. Finally, the foundations of modern musical life were laid at this time.

The organization of the selections that follow is based on two assumptions: on the one hand, that stylistic leadership rested with German and Austrian composers, although there were important contributions from elsewhere, notably France; and, on the other, that there was constant tension between the classical tradition, which basically accepted the forms of the past (i.e., the late eighteenth century), and the romantic tradition, which devised new ones for the present and future.

The anthology begins (Chapter 1: Weber, Schubert, Mendelssohn, Schumann) with the earliest music generally regarded as Romantic, composed by German and Austrian composers from around 1810 to 1840 or so. The work of these composers in some respects stayed close to the norms of the classical tradition, yet in others clearly pointed ahead; here, at all events, the decisive shift in repertory already described makes itself apparent. Next (Chapter 2: Berlioz, Chopin, Donizetti, Bellini, Meyerbeer) are examples of music from France and Italy, where one finds both progressive and conservative tendencies, the latter especially in Italian opera. Returning to Germany and Austria, there is a middle phase (Chapter 3: Liszt, Wagner, Brahms, Bruckner) from about 1840 to the 1880s (there is some overlapping), where the split between the by now fully developed new forms and those of the older tradition has become abundantly clear and moreover was recognized at the time (see the quotation from Liszt). Then the anthology turns once more to Italy and France for examples of opera and instrumental music from the early 1850s to the 1880s (Chapter 4: Verdi, Puccini, Franck, Bizet, Massenet), where the acceptance or rejection of the Germanic forms was an important issue. The next section (Chapter 5: Dvořák, Grieg, Mussorgsky, Tchaikovsky) provides examples of the music of the National Schools, mostly in Eastern Europe and Russia, which was characterized by efforts to establish indigenous forms in the face of the power and prestige of the Western, specifically Germanic, tradition. Finally (Chapter 6: Wolf, Mahler, Strauss), there are examples of German and Austrian music at the end of the century (and the beginning of the next), where generally the specifically Romantic tendencies have been elaborated and even exaggerated in the pursuit of ever more intense, powerful, and novel forms of expression.

1

The Early Phase in Germany and Austria

What generally is recognized as Romantic music commenced in the second and third decades of the nineteenth century, shortly after the death of Haydn and with much of Beethoven's most important work yet to come. Although there had indeed been examples of music in the eighteenth century in which the element of expression had been equal to, if not more important than, other aspects of composition—by C. P. E. Bach, Haydn, and Mozart[1]—it is at this time that the shift in repertory to the smaller forms, the emphasis on lyricism and sonority, and the association of musical compositions with extramusical aspects can be clearly discerned. This first took place mostly in Germany and Austria, the locus of the classical tradition, where the ground had been prepared in the field of literature. The composers and works chosen are representative of these trends. Carl Maria von Weber (1786–1826), a composer, pianist, conductor, and author, brought together for the first time many of the chief subjects and symbols of German literary Romanticism in his opera *Der Freischütz*. Franz Peter Schubert (1797–1828), one of the first composers who has not himself a professional instrumentalist or singer, not only composed large-scale instrumental pieces but also established the art song and the character piece as leading genres of composition. Felix Mendelssohn (1809–1847), composer, conductor, pianist, and administrator, combined literary associations with forms belonging to the classical tradition, while also working with the shorter forms. Finally, Robert Schumann, (1810–1856), pianist, composer, conductor, and man of letters, emphasized the smaller forms, especially in the early part of his career—his later work gives prominence to the large forms of instrumental music—all set forth in a highly individual style.

---

[1] See MCP, No. 5 (Bach), 8 (Haydn), and 20 (Mozart); in other anthologies: Bach in MSO and NAWM; Haydn in MSO; and Mozart in AMA (Fantasia).

Section One: Weber

Selections from *Der Freischütz* (J. 277)[1], Act II

A. "Wie nahte mir der Schlummer," Recitative and Aria
B. Finale (Wolf's Glen Scene)

The opera *Der Freischütz*, Weber's principal work, displays at one stroke the most typical features of German Romanticism. Completed in 1820, with a libretto by Friedrich Kind, the opera is set during the Middle Ages in the depths of a forest. Its plot involves Max, a young huntsman, who in his desire to win the shooting match and thus the hand of Agathe, the gamekeeper's daughter, resorts to magic bullets (*Freikugeln*) that have the property of always striking their target. But these bullets can only be obtained from Samiel, the Black Hunter (the Devil), for whom the last of them is reserved. Thus, the plot combines the Romantic interests in the long ago and faraway, nature (the forest), the supernatural, and folklore. The story clearly also has elements in common with the Faust legend.

Two elemental forces are effectively contrasted in the work: nature, as in the popular, folk-like music of the hunters, especially clear in the choral and dancing scenes and in the evocative use of the horns in the overture; and the demonic, characterized by the ominous theme associated with Samiel. This last features the tritone, long used to symbolize the devil (*diabolus in musica*), with dull pizzicati in the bass against a sustained chord in the winds.

Der Freischütz owes much to the German *Singspiel* tradition[2]—there is spoken dialog and a number of the arias are songs (*Lieder*) in strophic form. Yet it employs recitative and some of the arias exhibit the complex formal arrangements that came with the abandonment of the strict separation of recitative and aria that had been prevalent in Baroque opera. Similar arrangements may be found in the Italian opera of the time. An example is "Wie nahte mir der Schlummer," Agathe's big aria in Act II. While it is described in the score as recitative and aria, it really is much more: a free succession of recitative and aria-like elements that cannot be encompassed by any traditional musical scheme. The following provides a guide to the selection. Agathe, in her room, awaits the arrival of Max and looks out at the woods at night:

- Recitative, E, "Wie nahte mir der Schlummer"
- Lullaby, Strophe I (b. 17)
- Recitative (b. 35)
- Lullaby, Strophe II (b. 41)
- Andante, C (b. 61), arioso

---

[1] "J" numbers have been assigned to Weber's works by F. W. Jahns, *Carl Maria von Weber in seinen Werken* (Berlin: Schlesinger, 1871; 2nd ed., Berlin-Lichterfeld: Lienau, 1891/R 1967).
[2] See MCP, 394.

- Recitative (b. 76)
- Vivace con fuoco, E (b. 107)

Throughout the excerpt, musical elements highlight aspects of the drama. Harmonic changes, particularly the coloristic tertian progessions, are prominent. A telling one may be found in the first recitative, where Weber moves from B through an incomplete statement of the b triad to G, implying a cadence to C, but instead unexpectedly returning to B at "Welch' schöne Nacht" (b. 10–15). Thus the change in the text is matched by one in the music. A similar move, this time from E to C, comes after the second strophe of the Lullaby. In the Andante (b. 61), the rush of figuration symbolizes the beating of Agathe's heart as well as the motion of the breeze. Finally, typical of the work as a whole is the range of styles, from the folk-like to the operatic: The former is represented by the Lullaby, with its regular phrase structure (four-bar units), homophony, and predominantly syllabic declamation, the latter by the Vivace at the end, where Agathe's ecstatic exultation is rendered by brilliant figuration and sustained high notes. The melody used here, incidentally, has appeared earlier as the secondary theme of the overture.[3]

The "Wolf's Glen" scene, where the magic bullets are cast, is one of the most celebrated passages in all Romantic opera. It also serves as the finale to Act II. Following eighteenth-century tradition, it is organized as a long sectional ensemble with increasing activity near the end. The characters include Kaspar, who has persuaded Max to come for the magic bullets, Samiel (a speaking role), and Max. The scene may be outlined as follows:

Bar	Outline
1	Sostenuto, *ff*. Note the effective orchestration (somber chords in the brass accompanied by tremolo in the strings, along with the graphic shrieking of the owl [piccolo] and offstage chorus). This leads to Kaspar's invocation of Samiel (emphasis on repeated notes using but few different note values, in the style reserved for oracular pronouncements and the like in eighteenth-century opera).
51	Agitato, *c*. Kaspar and Samiel, the latter introduced by his characteristic theme. Kaspar's part is written in the parlante style,[4] while Samiel speaks, so that the section is, at least in part, a melodrama.[5]
110	Allegro, *c*. Kaspar awaits Max. When Max arrives, Kaspar adopts Samiel's mode (melodrama) while Max sings (recitative); Max sees visions of his mother and Agathe.

[3] The Overture, along with Max's aria "Doch mich umgarnen finstere Mächte," is in *NAWM*.

[4] *Parlante* is a variety of recitative in which musically the leading role is given to the orchestra, usually in the form of a figure or motive that is dominant in the accompaniment; the sung parts are assigned inconsequential melodic material, dominated by leaps, triadic figures, and repeated notes, in short phrases. The tempo is ordinarily fast. See the discussion in J. Kerman, *Opera as Drama* (New York: Vintage, 1965), 136 ff.

[5] *Melodrama* or *monodrama* was used in the eighteenth century to describe a dramatic piece or part of a piece in which spoken dialogue is accompanied as if it were sung recitative. Popularized by Rousseau and J. Benda, it was used by Beethoven in *Fidelio* and the music for *Egmont*.

Bar	Outline
261	Andante (later Allegro moderato and Presto), c. The casting of the bullets, preceded by spoken dialogue and set in part as *melodrama*. The actual casting of the bullets is presented as an accumulation with crescendo in stages, the counting of each bullet followed by a ghostly echo. At the last bullet, the main theme of the overture is presented (b. 373). When Samiel appears near the end, the harmony shifts from c to f♯, where it concludes, as the clock strikes one. The presence of a clock here in the center of the forest is not explained.

The passage at the beginning of the scene illustrates Weber's emphasis on sonority. Along with the evocative scoring (see the preceding discussion), coloristic harmonies form a "little harmonic labyrinth" within the context of f♯. Weber achieves this through a series of nonfunctional diminished and dominant-seventh chords over a chromatically descending bass. The passage simultaneously culminates and resolves with the dominant-seventh chord in C♯ that leads back to f♯.

TRANSLATION[1]

B. FINALE

(A terrible forest glen, planted mostly with pines, surrounded by high mountains. A waterfall rushes down from one of them. The full moon shines with a pale light. Thunderstorms approach from two directions. In the front a tree struck by lightning and withered and decayed inside so that it seems to glow. On the other side, on a gnarled branch sits a large bird with eyes of fire that roll. Crows and other woodbirds on other trees. Kaspar, without hat or coat but with hunting sack and knife, is busy laying out a circle of stones in the middle of which is a skull; a few paces away are the wings of an eagle, a casting-ladle and a mold for bullets.)

Chorus of Invisible Spirits:
  Moonmilk fell on weeds! Uhui!
  Spider's web is bedewed with blood!
    Uhui!
  Before evening falls again—Uhui!

The gentle bride will be dead. Uhui!
Before night falls again—Uhui!
The sacrifice will have been complete. Uhui! Uhui! Uhui!

(The clock strikes twelve in the distance. The stone circle is complete. Kaspar rips his hunting knife out and stabs the skull with it, turns around three times and calls.)

Kaspar:
  Samiel, Samiel, appear!
  By the sorcerer's skull,
  Samiel, Samiel, appear.

Samiel (spoken throughout):
  Why do you call me?

Kaspar:
  You know that my term is almost over.

Samiel:
  Tomorrow!

Kaspar:
  Extend it for me once more.

[1] English translation by William S. Mann, ©1960. Reprinted by kind permission of Deutsche Grammophon Production/Polydor International GmbH, Hamburg, and Mr. Mann. The stage directions have been cut somewhat, and other slight modifications have been made.

Samiel:
>No!

Kaspar:
>I can bring you a new sacrifice.

Samiel:
>Which one?

Kaspar:
>My hunting companion. He is
>coming.
>He has never entered your dark
>kingdom.

Samiel:
>What does he want?

Kaspar:
>Magic bullets, on which he builds
>his hopes.

Samiel:
>Six will hit, seven make a fool of
>him.

Kaspar:
>The seventh is yours! Aim it from
>his barrel to his bride.
>Despair will make him yours.
>Him—and the father—

Samiel:
>I have no stake in her yet.

Kaspar:
>Is he alone sufficient for you?

Samiel:
>We shall see!

Kaspar:
>But you will give me another term.
>And for another three years. I'll
>bring him to you as your prey!

Samiel:
>So be it. By the gates of Hell,
>tomorrow, he or you!

(Samiel disappears.)

Kaspar (spoken from here to the end of
the scene):
>Excellent service! Blessings on you,
>Samiel. He has made me warm.
>But where is Max? Is he going to
>break his word? Samiel, help me!

Max (above):
>Ah! Fearful yawns
>the gloomy chasm. What a horror!
>My eyes seem to be
>gazing into a swamp of hell!
>See how the storm clouds are
>gathering there.
>The moon has lost its shine;
>ghostly mist-shapes shimmer.
>The rock itself seems alive.
>And over there, quiet, quiet,
>night-birds fly up in the bushes.
>Branches, red-grey and scarred,
>stretch
>out gigantic arms to me!
>No! Though my heart be horrified,
>I must go on—I defy all terrors!

Kaspar:
>Thanks, Samiel. My term has been
>extended. Have you come at last,
>comrade? Was it right for you to
>leave me alone so long? Don't you
>see how distasteful all this is for
>me?

(He has been fanning the fire with the
eagle's wing, which he points at Max.)

Max:
>I shot the eagle from high in the air;
>I cannot turn back—destiny calls.
>Woe is me. I can't get down.

Kaspar:
>Come on, we're losing time. Rabbit!
>You usually climb like a sheep.

Max:
>Look over there! Look!

(He points to the rock: a form veiled in
white raising its hand is seen.)

What appears there
is my mother's ghost.
Thus she lay in her coffin, thus she
    rests in her grave.
With a look of warning she begs me,
    she waves me to go back!

Kaspar:

Help me, Samiel! Stupid ideas! Ha
    ha! Look again and you'll see
    what comes of your stupidity and
    cowardice.

(The veiled form has vanished and
Agathe's form is seen, with hair in disar-
ray and strangely adorned with leaves
and straw. She is like an insane person
and appears on the point of hurling herself into the waterfall.)

Max:

Agathe! she's going to jump into the
    water!
I must go down! I must!

(The image vanishes.)

Kaspar:

I think so too.

Max:

Here I am! What have I got to do?

Kaspar:

First, have a drink. The night air is
    cold and damp. Will you make
    the casts yourself?

Max:

No, that is against our agreement.
    What have I got to do, sorcerer?

Kaspar:

Have courage. Whatever you see or
    hear, keep quiet. If someone
    unknown to you should appear
    and help us, makes no difference
    to you. But if something else
    should come, so what? You won't
    be able to see it anyway.

Max:

How will all this come out?

Kaspar:

Death is in vain. Hidden beings do
    not give their treasures up to
    mortals easily. Only if you see me
    trembling, then come and help
    me, and call out what I call out, or
    else we're both lost.

Be quiet. Every moment is precious.
    Watch me so that you can learn
    the art. First the lead—some
    ground glass from broken church
    windows; you can find that.
    Some quicksilver. Three bullets
    that have hit their targets. The
    right eye of a hoopoe, the left one
    of a lynx. Probatum est. Now the
    blessing of the bullets.

Protect us, you who watch in the
    dark!

Samiel, Samiel, hear us.

Stand by my side in this night
    until the spell has been completed.
    Bless for me the herb and lead,
    bless them by seven, nine and three,
    that the bullet will be worthy.

Samiel, Samiel, come to me!

(The mixture in the kettle begins to
foment and bubble and gives off a green-
white glow. A cloud passes over the
moon, so that the area is lit only by the
fire, the owl's eyes and the stump of the
rotten tree.)

Kaspar (pouring the bullets):

One!

Echo:

One.

(Woodbirds fly down, settle around the
circle, hop and flutter.)

Kaspar:

Two!

Echo:
> Two.

(A black boar crashes through the bushes and chases on.)

Kaspar:
> Three!

Echo:
> Three.

(A storm rises, bends and breaks the tops of the trees and blows sparks from the fire.)

Kaspar:
> Four!

Echo:
> Four.

(A rushing is heard, cracking of whips and trampling of horses; four fiery wheels roll past, throwing off sparks.)

Kaspar:
> Five!

Echo:
> Five.

(Barking of dogs and neighing in the air; misty forms of hunters on foot and horseback, stags and dogs, fly by overhead.)

Chorus (invisible):
> Over hill, over dale, through abyss
>   and pit,
> over dew and clouds, tempest and
>   night,
> over cave, swamp and void,
> through fire, earth, sea and air
> yahoo, way, away, ho ho!

Kaspar:
> Alas! the pack of wild hunters!
> Six!

Echo:
> Six.

(The whole sky turns black as night; the storms come together horribly; the earth spouts fire; will-o'-the wisps appear on the mountains, etc.)

Kaspar:
> Samiel, Samiel, Samiel! Help!
> Seven!

Max:
> Samiel!

(At this moment the storm begins to abate and in place of the rotten tree stands the Black Huntsman, reaching for Max's hand.)

Samiel:
> Here I am!

(Max makes the sign of the cross and falls to the ground. The clock strikes one.)

WEBER: *Der Freischütz*, Act II, Recitative and Aria, "Wie nahte mir der Schlummer" (J. 277)

WEBER: *Der Freischütz*, Act II, Finale (Wolf's Glen Scene) (J. 277)

(Die verschleierte Gestalt ist verschwunden, man erblickt Agathens Gestalt mit aufgelösten Locken und wunderlich mit Laub und Stroh aufgeputzt. Sie gleicht einer Wahnsinnigen, und scheint in dem Begriff, sich in den Wasserfall hinab zu stürzen.)

258

Caspar (wirft ihm die Jagdflasche zu, die Max weg-legt). Zuerst trink' einmal! Die Nachtluft ist kühl und feucht. Willst du selbst giessen?
Max. Nein, das ist wider die Abrede.
Caspar. Nicht? So bleib' ausser dem Kreise, sonst kostet's dein Leben!
Max. Was hab' ich zu thun. Hexenmeister?
Caspar. Fasse Muth! Was du auch hören und sehen magst, verhalte dich ruhig.(Mit eigenem heim-lichen Grausen.) Käme vielleicht ein Unbekannter, uns zu helfen, was kümmert's dich? Kommt was an-ders, was thut's?— So etwas sieht ein Gescheiter gar nicht!
Max. O, wie wird das enden!
Caspar. Umsonst ist der Tod! Nicht ohne Wi-derstand schenken verborgene Naturen den Sterb-lichen ihre Schätze. Nur wenn du mich selbst zit-tern siehst, dann komme mir zu Hülfe und rufe,was ich rufen werde, sonst sind wir beide verloren.
Max.(macht eine Bewegung des Einwurfs.)
Caspar. Still! Die Augenblicke sind kostbar! (Der Mond ist bis auf einen schmalen Streif verfinstert. Caspar nimmt die Giesskelle.) Merk' auf, was ich hin-ein werfen werde, damit du die Kunst lernst! (Er nimmt die Ingredienzen aus der Jagdtasche und wirft sie nach und nach hinein.)

261

Caspar. Hier erst das Blei! Etwas gestossenes Glas von zerbrochenen Kirchenfenstern; das findet sich. Et-was Quecksilber. Drei Kugeln, die schon einmal getroffen.

Das rechte Auge ei-nes Wiedehopfs, das linke eines Luchses! Probatum est!

Und nun den Kugelsegen!

(In drei Pausen sich gegen die Erde neigend.)

267

Caspar. Schütze, der im Dunkeln wacht, Sa-miel! Samiel! Hab'   acht, steh' mir bei in dieser   Nacht,bis der Zauber ist voll-   bracht. Salbe mir so Kraut als

310

Corni in F.

Corni in E.

Trombe.

Timp.

(Die Gewitter treffen furchtbar zusammen. Flammen schlagen aus der Erde. Irrlichter zeigen sich auf den Bergen u.s.w.)

384

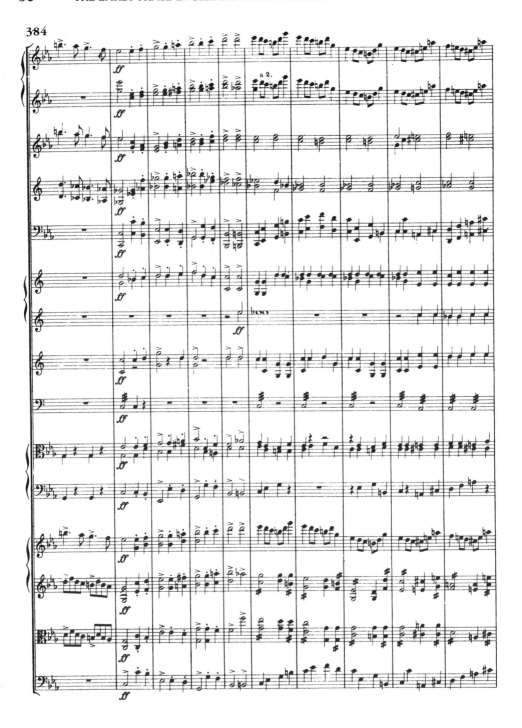

394

404

Caspar.
Samiel!   hilf!
(Er wird zu Boden geworfen).

Max (gleichfalls vom Sturm hin- und herge-
schleudert, springt aus dem Kreis, fasst einen
Ast des verdorrten Baums und schreit):
Sieben!   Samiel!
(In demselben Augenblicke fängt das Un-
gewitter an, sich zu beruhigen, an der Stelle
des verdorrten Baums steht der schwarze
Jäger, nach Maxens Hand fassend).

Samiel (mit furcht-
barer Stimme):
Hier bin ich!

Max (schlägt ein
Kreuz und stürzt
zu Boden).

416

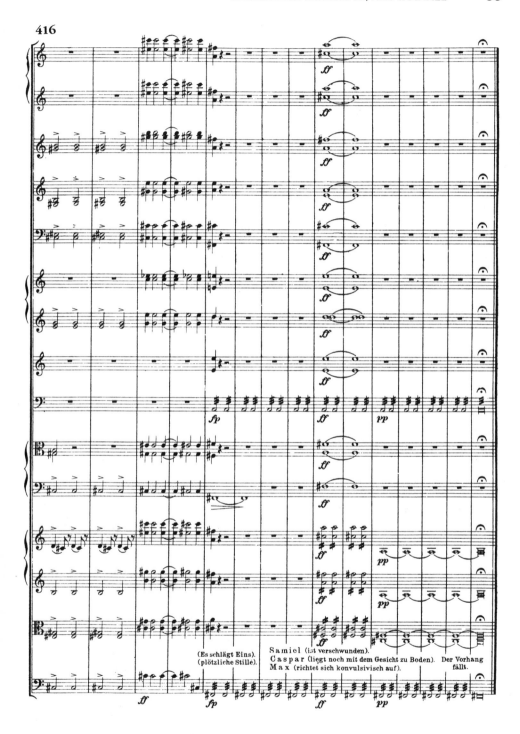

(Es schlägt Eins).　　Samiel (ist verschwunden).
(plötzliche Stille).　Caspar (liegt noch mit dem Gesicht zu Boden).　Der Vorhang
　　　　　　　　　Max (richtet sich konvulsivisch auf).　　　　fällt.

Section Two: Schubert

Songs

A. "Gretchen am Spinnrade" (D. 118/op. 2)[1]
B. "Nähe des Geliebten" (D. 162/op. 5, no. 2)
C. "Prometheus" (D. 674)
D. "Der Lindenbaum," from *Winterreise* (D. 911/op. 89, no. 5)

"Gretchen am Spinnrade," composed October 19, 1814, is at once the first of Schubert's settings of Goethe and his first indisputably great song. In the poem, a dramatic soliloquy from *Faust*, Gretchen, who has fallen in love with Faust, reflects on all he means to her, as she sits at the spinning wheel. The repeated figure in the accompaniment symbolizes both the motion of the wheel and Gretchen's agitated state of mind. While the song is often regarded as essentially of the on-running or through-composed type, it has a refrain element, stated at the outset, between the episodes, and finally at the end, where it is most effectively broken off. Each episode brings an increasing intensity that eventually leads to a climax; moreover, with each episode the strength of the climax is increased. Particularly effective is the stopping of the spinning-wheel figure in the accompaniment after the second episode at "Ach! sein Kuss!" and its subsequent gradual and halting resumption. For the most part, Schubert stays in his main key, *d*, and those related to it (*a, E, F*). An individual touch, however, is the implication of *C* at the cadence. Harmonic instability comes with the song's third episode (b. 84 ff.) as Gretchen, beside herself, longs to "pass away in his kisses."

"Nähe des Geliebten," composed the following year also to a poem by Goethe, shows the strict strophic form, here with four strophes. The prevailing mood is of nocturnal calm, as suggested by the constant triplet motion, the predominantly diatonic harmonies, and the relative lack of dissonance. Yet the unusual prelude does not begin in the main key (*Gb*), but in *Bb*, only to work its way to the tonic, which arrives via a diminished-seventh chord, one of the few dissonances in the song.

"Prometheus," composed in 1819, is more ambitious. Here Schubert chose one of the most important poems from Goethe's *Sturm und Drang* period, a powerful monlogue of defiance by the rebel god Prometheus, himself a central symbol in Romantic art and literature. This song provides a good example of the sectional type of song with recitative passages, a type modeled on the operatic *scena*. The alternation between passages in recitative style and those in arioso style is clear in the song; an example of the latter, for instance, is at b. 42 ("Da ich ein Kind war"). Orchestra-like accompaniment is suggested by the frequent use of tremolo and the many full chords in the piano. Apart from the analogy to opera, the free form of the song accords with

---

[1] The "D" numbers are those assigned to Schubert's work in O. E. Deutsch, *Franz Schubert: Verzeichnis seiner Werke in zeitlicher Folge* (Kassel: Bärenreiter, 1978); earlier ed. in English (New York: Norton, 1951).

that of Goethe's poem, which dispenses with both regular meter and rhyme. The song also does not preserve the usual consistency of key; it commences in *Bb* but concludes in *C*. For comparison, see Wolf's setting of the same poem (in Chapter 6).

The last example, "Der Lindenbaum," involves the song cycle, a series of songs that are related through their texts, often, but not always, presenting a narrative. This song comes from the cycle *Winterreise*, for which Schubert used poems by Wilhelm Müller, who also wrote the poems used in Schubert's earlier cycle, *Die schöne Müllerin* (D. 795/op. 25). *Winterreise* portrays the solitary winter journey of a rejected suitor, in which sorrow, remembrance, and hope are mingled. The journey ends in insanity and—by implication—death. In "Der Lindenbaum," the most familiar song in the cycle, the wanderer's past happiness is contrasted with his plight in the present. Schubert employs the modified strophic form in conjunction with a melody modeled on folk song, though changes are made in the accompaniment from strophe to strophe, not the least of them being an alternation between major and minor.[2] The departure from strophic form occurs in the setting of the poem's fifth strophe, corresponding to the agitation in the text. In the first part of the song, Schubert combined two strophes of Müller's poem to make a single musical strophe. But in the third strophe, where the mood change takes place, Schubert used but one of Müller's strophes (the fifth) to produce a musical one that is shorter than the others (8 bars, as opposed to 16). In order to make a concluding strophe of the same length as his first, Schubert had to set the text of Müller's last (sixth) strophe twice. Note the evocative "horn" fifths at the beginning of the song (repeated later), as well as the graphic representation of the cold wind blowing away the wanderer's hat, once more introduced by a tertian progression (*E–C*).[3]

TRANSLATIONS

A. GRETCHEN AT THE SPINNING WHEEL

Refrain
> My peace is gone,
> my heart is heavy,
> I'll never, never,
> find peace again.

Strophe 1
> Whenever I am without him
> is to me like the grave;
> the whole world
> has turned sour.

Strophe 2
> My poor head
> has gone crazy;
> my poor senses
> are scattered in bits and pieces.

Repeat Refrain

Strophe 3
> I seek him alone
> when I look to the window;
> I leave the house
> only to go to him.

---

[2] Müller's poems were also based on folk song, particularly as represented in the influential anthology *Des Knaben Wunderhorn* (published 1805–1808).

[3] Other songs in anthologies: "Der Erlkönig" is in AMA and NSe and "Der Doppelgänger" in AMA and CSM; "Was ist Sylvia?" is in AMA and "Wohin?" in CSM; "Heidenröslein," "Die Forelle," and "Der Tod und das Mädchen" are all in MSO.

Strophe 4

    His broad bearing,
    his noble form,
    the smile of his mouth
    and the power of his eyes;

Strophe 5

    and the magic flow
    of his speech,
    the pressure of his hand
    and, ah, his kiss!

Repeat Refrain

Strophe 6

    My bosom urges
    toward him.
    Ah! if I could but seize
    and hold him!

Strophe 7

    And kiss him
    as much as I want,
    that I might pass away
    in his kisses.

Repeat Refrain (incomplete)

B. NEARNESS OF THE BELOVED

Strophe 1

    I think of you when the sun's
      shimmer
    comes to me from the sea;
    I think of you when the shining
      moon paints
    itself in the brook.

Strophe 2

    I see you when on a distant path
      the dust clouds rise;
    in the deep night, when on a narrow
      path
    the traveler trembles.

Strophe 3

    I hear you when there with muffled
      rumbling
    the wave raises up!

    in the quiet woods, where I often go
      to listen
    when all is quiet.

Strophe 4

    I am with you; though you are so far
      from me
    you are near me!
    The sun sets, soon the stars shine for
      me;
    oh, that you were here.

C. PROMETHEUS

    Cover your heavens, Zeus,
    with misty clouds
      and test yourself,
    like a boy who cuts off
    the heads of thistles,
    on the oaks and mountaintops.
    Yet you'll have to leave
    my Earth alone
    and my hut, which you did not
      build,
    and my hearth,
    whose glowing warmth
    you envy me.

    I know nothing more pitiful
    under the sun than you gods.
    You nourish yourself
    and your majesty meagerly
    on sacrificial offerings
    and the breath of prayers;
    and would even starve
    were children and beggars
    not hopeful fools.

    When I was a child
    and knew nothing of anything,
    I turned my errant eyes
    to the sun, as if there were
    up there an ear to hear my complaint,
    a heart, like mine,
    to pity the afflicted.

    Who helped me
    against the titans' insolence?

Who saved me from death,
from slavery?
Have you not done all this by
    yourself,
holy glowing heart?
And you should glow, young and
    good,
deceived by a thought of salvation
for the one sleeping over there?

I honor you? What for?
Have you ever lessened the pain
of him that is burdened?
Have you ever stilled the tears
of him that is filled with fear?

Have I not been fashioned into a man
by almighty time
and eternal fate,
my masters and yours?
Did you think
I would come to hate life
and flee into the deserts
because not all
my dream-blossoms grew ripe?

Here do I sit, forming men
after my own image,
a race that is like me,
to suffer, to weep,
to enjoy and to be happy
and to pay you no heed,
like me!

D. THE LINDEN TREE

Strophe 1

    At the fountain in front of the gate
    there stands a linden tree.
    I dreamed beneath its shadow
    so many sweet dreams.

Strophe 2

    I cut in its bark
    so many a word of love,
    in joy and sorrow
    I always wanted to come there.

Strophe 3

    Today I also have to pass by
    in the depths of night;
    in the dark there I have
    closed my eyes.

Strophe 4

    And its branches rustled
    as if they were calling me,
    Come to me, young man
    here you will find peace.

Strophe 5

    The cold winds blew
    straight in my face,
    the hat flew from my head,
    but I did not turn.

Strophe 6

    Now I am many hours
    distant from that place;
    and constantly I hear it rustling,
    Here you would find peace.

SCHUBERT: "Gretchen am Spinnrade" (D. 118/op. 2)

SCHUBERT: "Nähe des Geliebten" (D. 162/op. 5, no. 2)

Ich höre dich, wenn dort mit dumpfem Rauschen
    Die Welle steigt!
Im stillen Hain, da geh' ich oft zu lauschen,
    Wenn alles schweigt.

Ich bin bei dir; du seist auch noch so ferne,
    Du bist mir nah!
Die Sonne sinkt, bald leuchten mir die Sterne.
    O, wärst du da!

SCHUBERT: "Prometheus" (D. 674)

SCHUBERT: *Winterreise*, "Der Lindenbaum" (D. 911/op. 89, no. 5)

String Quartet in *a* (D. 804/op. 29, no. 1)

Although Schubert worked with the shorter lyric forms that became the hallmark of Romantic music—particularly the art song, of which he composed well over 600—the large forms from the late eighteenth century found a prominent place in his repertory. In 1824 Schubert made this explicit in a letter in which he avowed the intention to "make his way" to "grand symphony" through the composition of string quartets (and, one could infer, piano sonatas and other types of chamber music).[1] His earlier efforts in instrumental music maintained the old style of the Viennese *galant*, with its vivacious entertaining quality, which indeed had been characteristic in the late eighteenth century.[2] But Schubert gave these early works his own emphasis on lyricism and color. Good examples are provided by the Symphony 5, B♭ (D. 485) and the popular "Trout" Quintet in A (D. 667/op. 114).[3]

In view of the central position that the genre occupied in the Classic period, it was natural for Schubert to turn to the string quartet in his pursuit of "grand symphony." The Quartet in *a*, composed and performed in 1824 (it was, unusually for Schubert, also published the same year), represents the first completed quartet along this path. It had been preceded by piano sonatas composed in 1818–1819 and 1823 as well as the impressive *Quartettsatz* (*Quartet Movement*), *c* (D. 703), presumably the first movement of a projected string quartet (a fragmentary slow movement survives), composed in 1820. These works all broke away from the *galant* aesthetic and strove for greater scope and intensity. In any case, this quartet shows the salient features of Schubert's art: the prominence of lyric themes, which, among other things, resulted in the lyrical interpretation of the sonata structure; the richness of the harmonies; and the emphasis given to tone color.

The quartet is cast in the traditional four-movement scheme: an Allegro ma non troppo in *a*, an Andante in C, the Minuetto in *a* with Trio in A, and, as finale, an Allegro moderato in A. The forms in these movements likewise correspond to what was traditional: sonata form with double bar in the first movement, a rondo-like arrangement with developmental episode in the second movement, the last statement of the principal section greatly altered, the usual Minuet and Trio in the third, and another rondo in the fourth.

Lyricism is evident throughout, as already indicated. As expected, it dominates the second movement, in this case with a theme borrowed by Schubert from the third entr'acte of *Rosamunde* (D. 797).[4] But it is less usual, although by no means unprecedented, to find such lyricism in the principal theme of a movement in the sonata structure. Here we have a long, tonally closed, melancholy melodic utterance in the violin I, to which the other instruments provide accompaniment. This theme, that is

---

[1] Letter to Leopold Kupelwieser, March 31, 1824; see *The Schubert Reader*, ed. O. Deutsch (New York: Norton, 1947), 456.

[2] MCP, 2–3.

[3] Excerpts in MSO and NSe.

[4] Several of Schubert's instrumental works have movements explicitly based on songs: the famous "Trout" Quintet, the "Wanderer" Fantasia for piano in C (D. 760) and the String Quartet in *d* (D. 810), to name the most well known. Less explicit associations between instrumental pieces and songs, which Einstein refers to as "affinities," have also been suggested.

to say, is set exactly like a song and could easily be imagined as a setting for voice and piano. Other prominent themes in the quartet are similar: the secondary theme of the first movement, for instance, is a duet for violins with accompaniment by viola and cello. We can point to the main themes of other movements as well. As is typical of Schubert, the development of the first movement proceeds by phrase and not by motive, as would have been characteristic, say, of the first movement of a quartet by Haydn.

In such a primarily lyric art, it is natural that thematic variation (thematic transformation or metamorphosis, as it came to be known) would be significant. In the first movement the transition theme clearly is derived from the beginning of the principal theme, but the secondary theme proves important as well, since it provides thematic material for the rest of the exposition. This last had indeed been prescribed for sonata structure by Czerny in his general account of the form.[5]

There is even a suggestion of cyclic form in the quartet, when at the end of the developmental episode in the last movement there is an abrupt halt that leaves the solo cello playing long and sustained C's that are ornamented by grace notes, clearly recalling the beginning of the Minuet. Moreover, the emphasis on keys related to *a* and on melodic lyricism throughout the quartet provide additional consistency.

The major feature of the work is its sonority, which in a string quartet is achieved principally through harmonies, part writing, and use of register. The song-like disposition of the themes is in itself an important factor, as already indicated. Two instances of coloristic harmony in the first movement may be mentioned. The first occurs in the retransition (b. 140), which is based on the principal theme. First, the diminished-seventh chord on $G\sharp$ is transformed through the enharmonic relation $G\sharp = A\flat$ and the flatting of B to the dominant-seventh chord on $B\flat$. Continuing with one short disturbance (at b. 155–57) on the flat side, Schubert returns to the original key via $E\flat = D\sharp$ and $G\sharp = F\sharp$. The bass then descends chromatically to reach the tonic 6/4 chord that ushers in the recapitulation. The second example is in the coda, with its expressive sevenths and ninths. Many other instances, such as the tritones at the first retransition to the main theme in the slow movement, can be identified. An individualizing feature of the first movement's principal theme is the alternation between major and minor, known as *molldur*. Another individual touch is the beginning of the Minuet, with its striking gapped texture: the inner parts close together and the outer ones far apart, introduced by an ornamented drone in the cello. A dance-like figure follows, and the subsequent alternation of the two creates a bittersweet effect. Similarities between this movement and the song "Die Götter Griechenlands" (D. 677) have been suggested, for instance by Einstein.[6]

The quartet thus presents a reinterpretation of the old genre. Size, scope, forms, and purpose remain the same, but the work is now infused with melodious themes, greater freedom of modulation, and new richness of color.[7]

---

[5] This was pointed out by M. Chusid in his edition of Schubert's "Unfinished" Symphony (NCS: New York, 1968), 71–74.

[6] Einstein, *Schubert, A Musical Portrait* (New York: Oxford, 1952), 252–53.

[7] Much the same thing is also found in his last String Quartet, G (D. 887/op. 161), the first movement of which is in CSM.

SCHUBERT: Quartet in *a* (D. 804/op. 29, no. 1)

MENUETTO.
Allegretto.

Impromptu in G♭ (D. 899/op. 90, no. 3)

Schubert's move to the shorter character piece for piano in 1823 with his *Moments musicals* (D. 780/op. 94)[1] accords with the shift in the repertory of art music that characterizes Romanticism. Schubert was no doubt specifically influenced by two Bohemian composers active in Vienna at the time, Vaclav Jan Tomášek and Jan Hugo Voříšek, especially the latter. For his character pieces, which for the most part were published either late in his life or posthumously, Schubert's publisher emphasized the symbolic designation *impromptu* (as if on the spur of the moment). These pieces are primarily lyric in conception and display the simple repetitive or reverting schemes often found in songs.

Typical here is the lyrical Andante in G♭ composed in 1827 (the original publisher had it transposed to G). The piece is in three-part form with coda. Throughout there is the song-like disposition, featuring a cantabile line over a standardized accompanimental figuration pattern and a supporting bass that at times takes on thematic significance, particularly in the midsection. This section, with its emphasis on the minor, provides the contrast. The sense of breadth and repose is in part at least the result of the unusual time signature (¢ ¢) that yields bars twice the normal length. Other factors include the prevailing regularity of phrase structure and the slow and regular harmonic rhythm established at the outset. These all contribute to the individual sound of the piece, in which the coloristic use of harmonies is paramount.

---

[1] With Einstein (*Schubert, A Musical Portrait* [New York: Oxford, 1952], 133) we retain Schubert's incorrect French.

SCHUBERT: Impromptu in G♭ (D. 899/op. 90, no. 3)

Section Three: Mendelssohn

Die Hebriden (op. 26)

Mendelssohn composed seven overtures, beginning with the epoch-making *A Mid-summer Night's Dream* (op. 21) in 1826.[1] *Die Hebriden* (*The Hebrides*, also known as *Fingal's Cave*),[2] was composed in 1830, revised in 1832, and premiered that same year in London. While its primary inspiration apparently came from Mendelssohn's trip to the Hebrides in 1829—he wrote his family that he had felt a "strange mood" there and included a draft of what came to be the principal theme of the work[3]—a literary component also seems likely: the allegedly primitive rhapsodic prose poems published by James Macpherson in the 1760s, which were attributed, for the most part falsely, to the ancient bard Ossian. Here the warrior Fingal (or Finn), who defended Ireland against the invading Danes, was an important character. The overture therefore combines two elements: the sea, particularly the graphic depiction of the motion of the waves, and heroism, suggested by the brass fanfares. The representation of landscape is common in Mendelssohn's work, as in the "Scotch" and "Italian" symphonies, and may reflect the fact that the composer was an accomplished artist who made many paintings and drawings, including one of the Hebrides Islands. Wagner referred to *Die Hebriden* as "a water-color by a great landscape painter,"[4] and the piece seems to have influenced his overture to *Der fliegende Holländer*.

Scored for the normal orchestra of the late eighteenth and early nineteenth centuries (18 parts: woodwinds and brass in pairs but excluding trombones, with timpani, and strings in five parts), *Die Hebriden*, in the key of *b*, follows the sonata structure but without the double bar. The form itself is articulated with great clarity: As would be expected, the prime elements are the principal theme, which represents the motion of the waves, the transition based on this theme (b. 26), the broadly lyrical secondary theme (b. 47), which Tovey characterized as "quite the greatest melody that Mendelssohn wrote,"[5] and the closing theme (b. 77). These—three distinct themes in all—dominate the development. Note the passage in which short figures in the winds are accompanied by changing harmonies in the strings (*tremolo*) in high register, testimony to the Romantic emphasis on sonority (b. 96 ff.). The recapitulation (b. 180) is shorter than the exposition. Throughout, the work is dominated by the principal theme, which appears in different guises, legato at first, then strongly accented, as in the closing theme, development, and coda, the last suggesting a storm. Mendelssohn's exploitation of this theme is another use of the technique of thematic transformation that plays such a significant role in Romantic music.

---

[1] The overture is reprinted in *NSe*, the scherzo in *NAWM*. Other pieces in the anthologies: Symphony 4, A (op. 90, "Italian") in *S* and the Violin Concerto, *e* (op. 64), complete in *C*, first movement alone in *NSe*, third movement alone in *MSO*.

[2] There is an earlier version of the overture with the title *Der einsame Insel*.

[3] Letter of August 7, 1829, quoted by E. Werner, *Mendelssohn: A New Image of the Composer and his Age* (New York: Free Press, 1963), 151.

[4] D. F. Tovey, *Essays in Musical Analysis*, iv (London: Oxford, 1936), 90.

[5] Ibid., 92. See also L. Todd, "Of Sea Gulls and Counterpoint: The Early Versions of Mendelssohn's *Hebrides* Overture," *19th Century Music*, 2 (1979): 197.

MENDELSSOHN: *Die Hebriden* (op. 26)

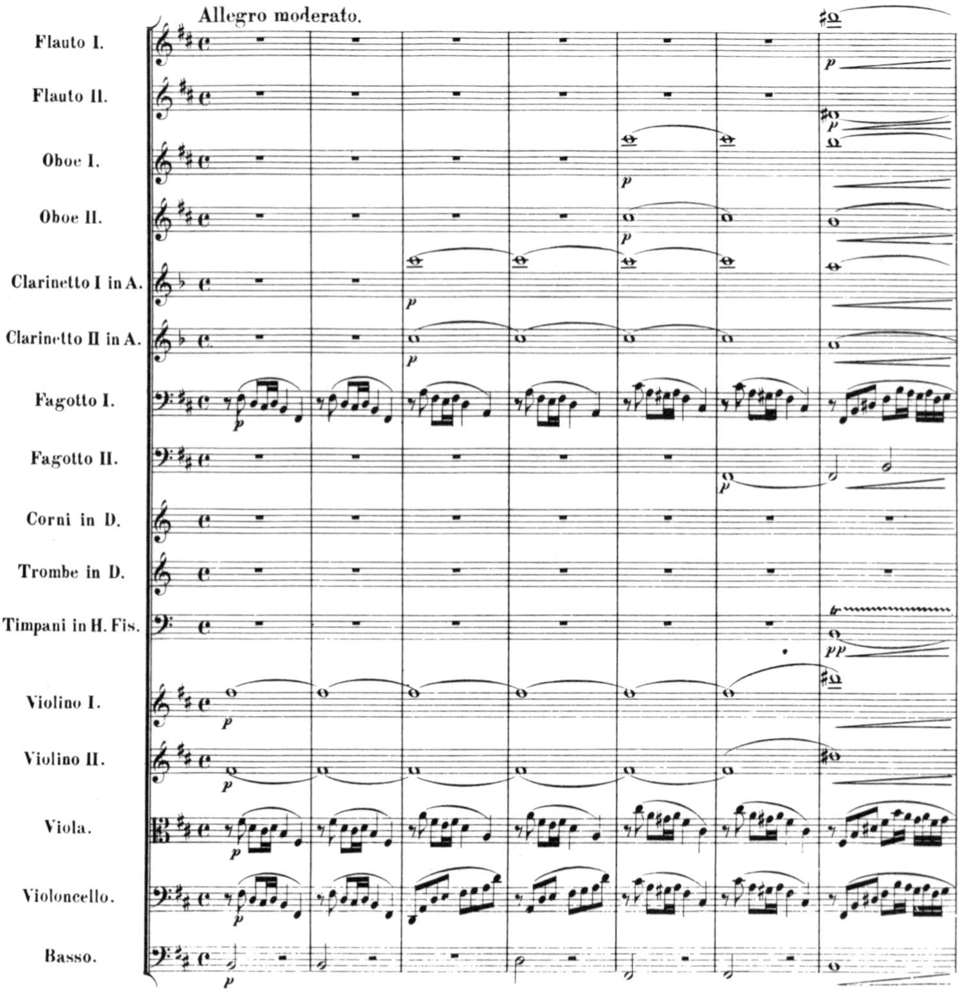

13

30

41

51

56

61

66

108

162

172

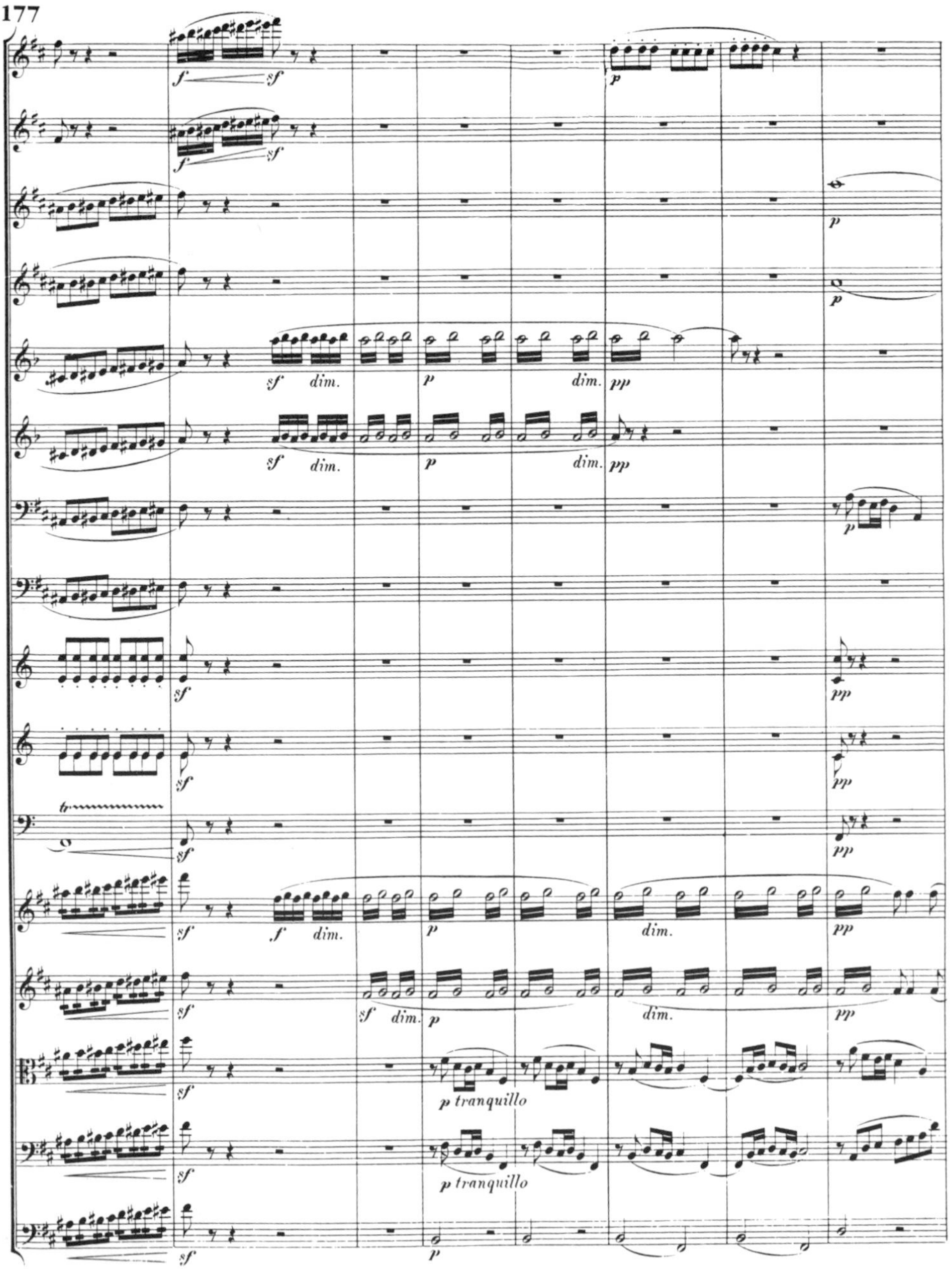
177
f
sf
sf dim.
p
dim. pp
tr
f dim.
p tranquillo
pp

185

191

200

213

220

225

230

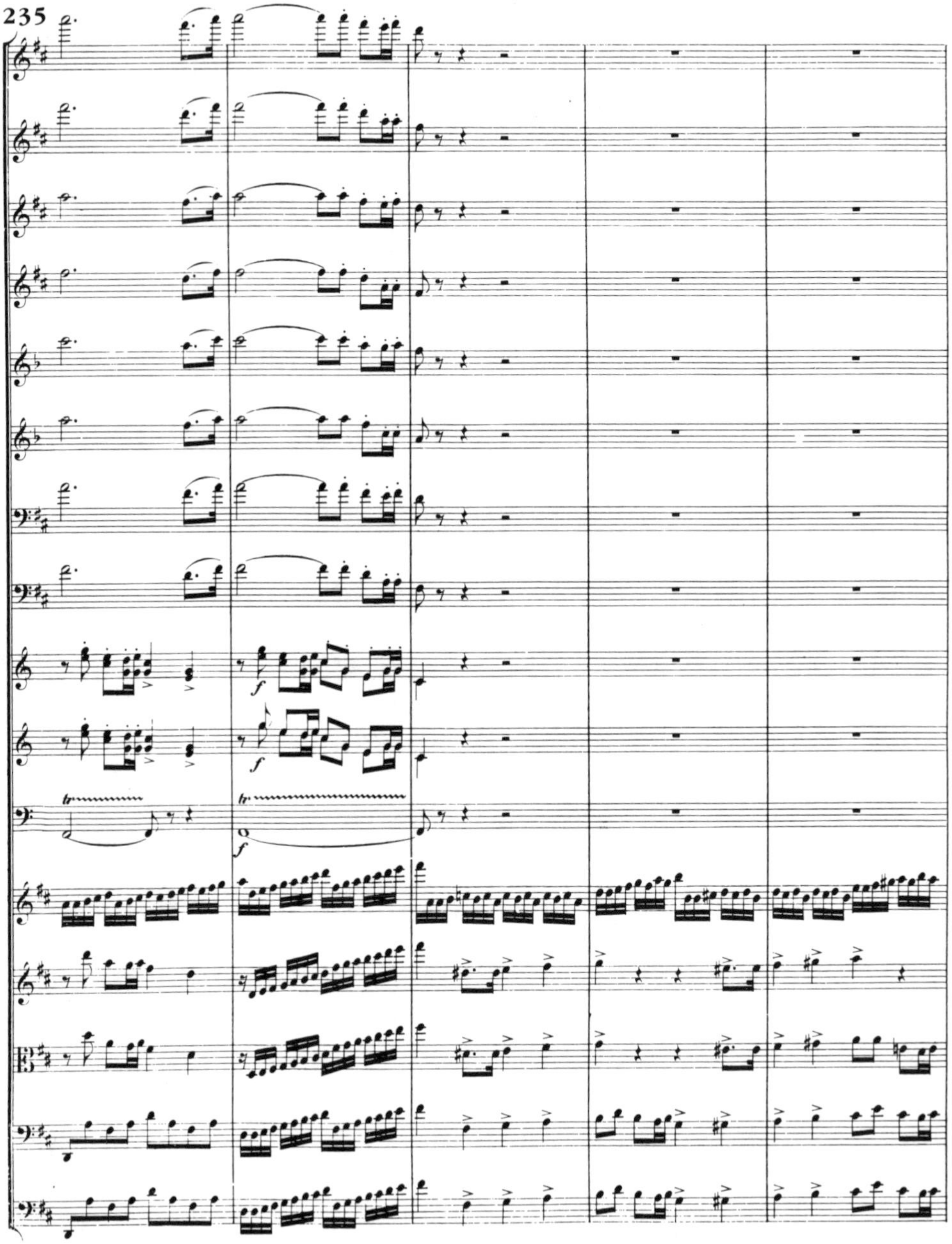
235

240

249

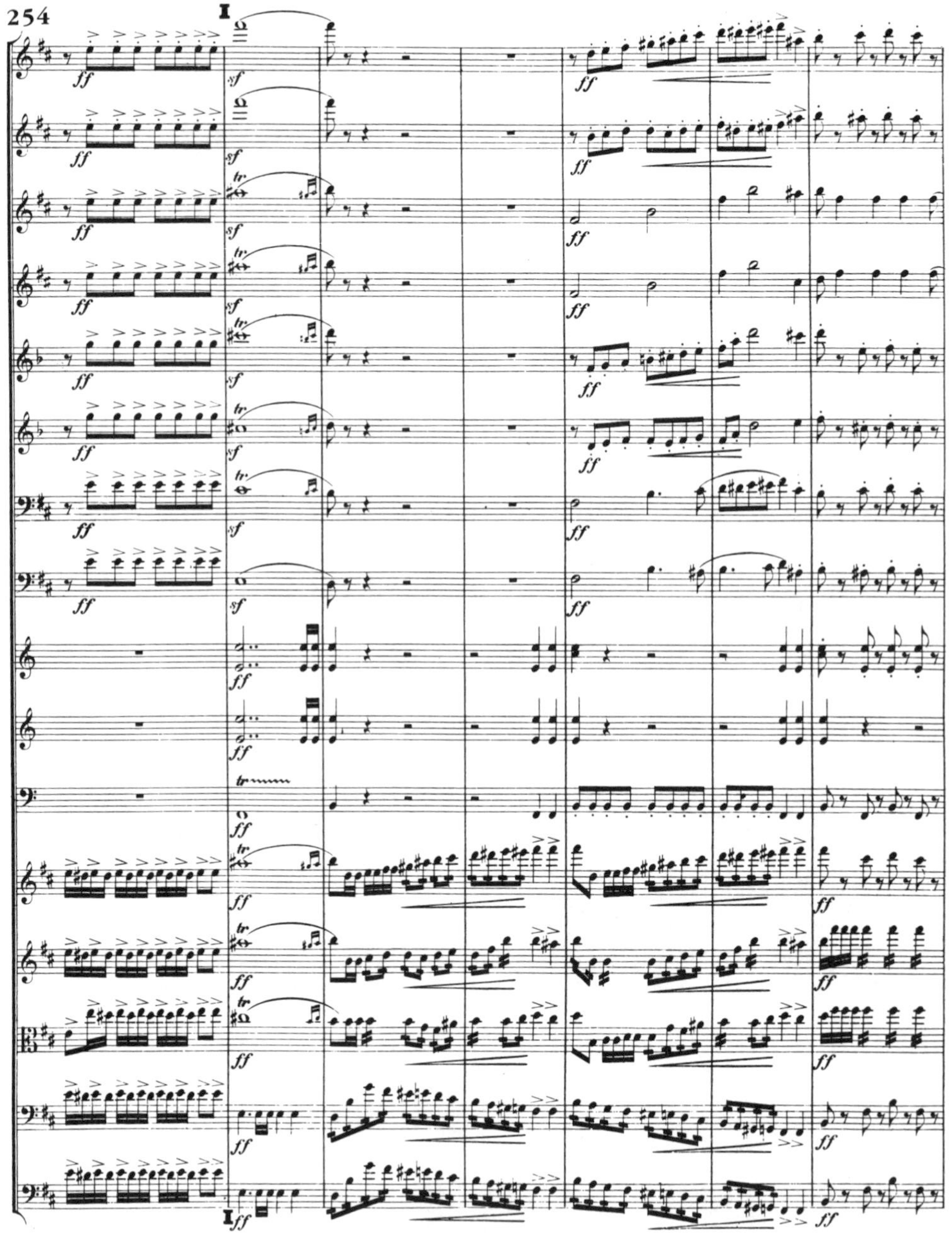
254
I
ff
sf
tr
I

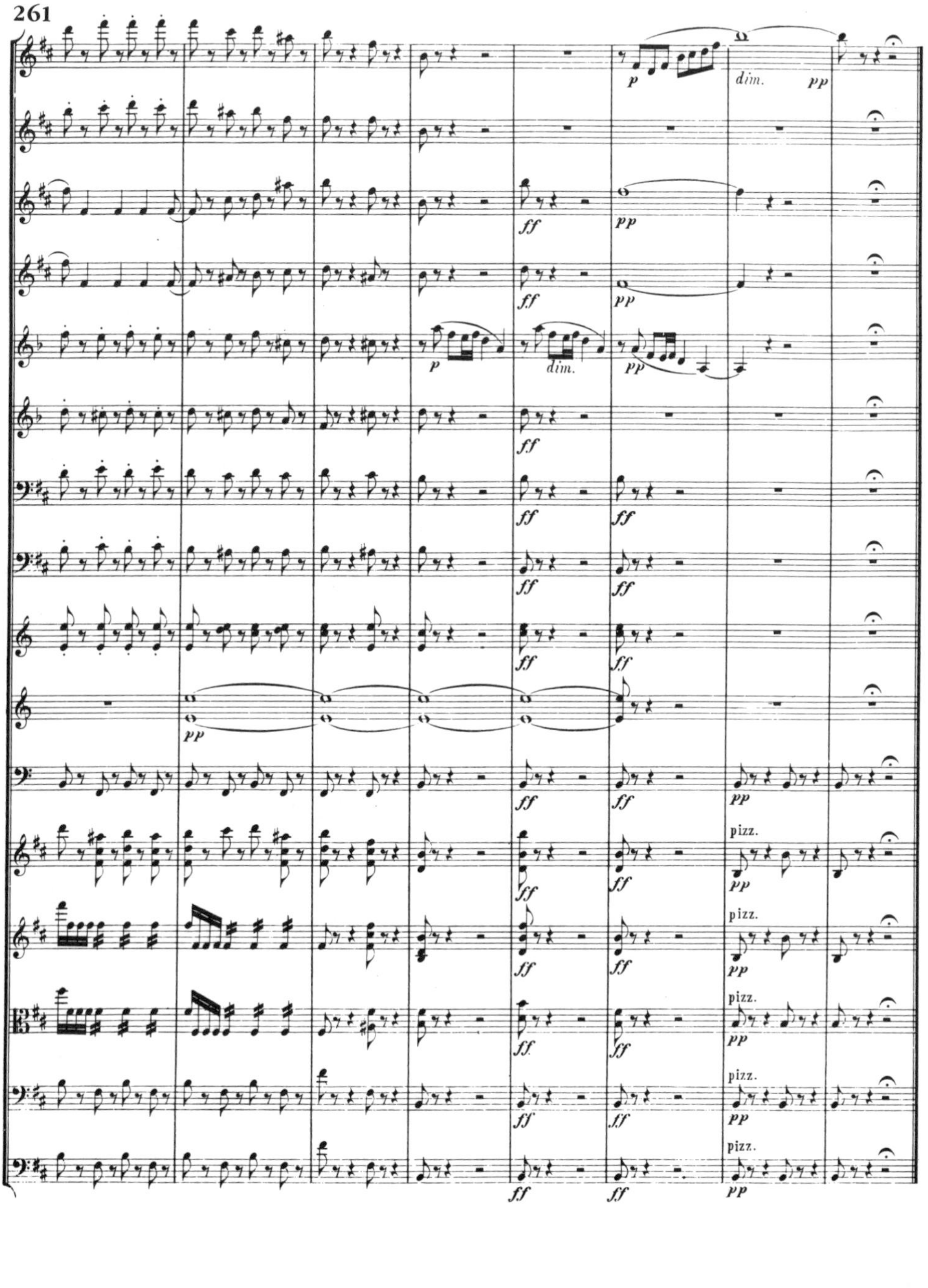
261
p
dim.
pp
ff
pizz.

Lieder ohne Worte (op. 62)

A. Andante espressivo in G (no. 1)
B. Allegro con fuoco in B♭ (no. 2)
C. Andante maestoso in e (no. 3)
D. Allegro con anima in G (no. 4)
E. Andante con moto in a (no. 5), "Venezianisches Gondellied"
F. Allegretto grazioso in A (no. 6)

Mendelssohn's principal contribution to the literature of the character piece consists of the eight sets of *Lieder ohne Worte* (*Songs without Words*), composed in the period 1829–1845, each of which contains six pieces. The title aptly symbolizes not only these pieces but the very nature of the character piece: a short lyrical piece—a song— but purely instrumental. As in songs, the left hand usually provides the accompaniment, which ordinarily consists of simple figurational patterns.

The six pieces included in op. 62, the fifth in the series, were composed in 1842–1844 and published in 1844. The titles used by Mendelssohn usually indicate tempo and character, but a few are more explicit and descriptive, as in the "Venetian Gondola Song" (no. 5), a barcarolle. The affects of others, however, have seemed clear enough, so that over time they have acquired titles: No. 3 has come to be known as the "Funeral March," and no. 6 as "Spring Song." Three song types common in early nineteenth-century Berlin, particularly in the repertory of Mendelssohn's teacher Zelter, provided models for these pieces: (1) the solo song with accompaniment (no. 1 and no. 6); (2) the duet with accompaniment (no. 5); and (3) the choral song (no. 4, the main section).[1]

As expected, the formal structures are for the most part simple and regular. Four types appear in op. 62; (1) the common three-part form, as in no. 4, with a passage serving as both introduction and coda, and an extra strain after the restatement of "a"; (2) the rondo with two episodes, as in no. 1 and no. 2, with the last statement of the rondo element appearing in the coda; (3) the elaboration of the standard scheme, "aaba," by the insertion of a passage between the "b" and the last statement of "a," as in no. 3; and (4) a binary arrangement in which the second part restates the first but with some changes, as in no. 6 (the second statement has been shortened). The exception is no. 5, the "Venetian Gondola Song," the structure of which is open to different interpretations. In view of the many associations between the *Lieder ohne Worte* and song types, it seems best to regard this piece as a varied strophic form, in which each strophe consists of three melodic elements ("a," "b," "c," but in the last strophe "d" replaces "c"). Each strophe is preceded by one or two descending fourths, perfect near the beginning and end, augmented in the middle. Moreover, an introduction includes two statements of the first strain ("a"), thus (In = Introduction; 4th = fourth(s); numerals = the strophes):

---

[1] See H. and L. Tischler, "Mendelssohn's Songs Without Words," MQ, 23 (1947): 1.

	In			1					2				3		
	4th	a	a	4th	a	a	b	c	4th	a	b	c	4th	a	b	d
Bar:	1	4	8	12	13	17	21	26	30	31	35	40	44	45	49	53

Contrast is not pronounced in these pieces. Indeed, no. 1 could almost serve as an example of the singleness of affect characteristic of Baroque music. Throughout the set, regularity of phrase structure prevails, while paired phrases and melodic sequences appear frequently.

Venetianisches Gondellied.

Section Four: Schumann

Selections from *Phantasiestücke* (op. 12)

    A. "Warum?" Db (no. 3)
    B. "Grillen," Db (no. 4)
    C. "In der Nacht, ƒ (no. 5)
    D. "Ende vom Lied," F (no. 8)

Before 1840 Schumann's composition was devoted almost exclusively to piano music, mostly character pieces. Usually published as sets, these pieces were intended either to be played consecutively, as in *Papillons* (op. 2) and *Carnaval* (op. 9), or individually, as in *Kreisleriana* (op. 16) and the set under consideration here. Each of the eight pieces in this set, which was composed in 1837 and published the following year, has a descriptive title, but, unlike many of Schumann's compositions, there appear to be no overt literary associations. The title of the set, however, may be related to a collection of stories by the writer E. T. A. Hoffmann (his *Phantasiestücke in Callots Manier*).

The collection provides a good example of Schumann's approach to the character piece.[1] The forms are simple: binary ("Warum?"), three-part ("In der Nacht" and "Ende vom Lied"), and rondo ("Grillen"), while repetitive structures, often binary, may be found in component passages as well. Lyricism predominates, but counterpoint also remains prominent, both in the accompaniment and in the presentation of the thematic material. Harmonically, the strength of the tonic is often undermined by consistent chromaticism, particularly the frequent use of secondary dominant-seventh chords, by beginning in a key other than the tonic ("Warum?" and "Grillen") and by stating tonally important chords in weak positions (inversions). A good example is "Ende vom Lied," where the tonic is not reached until b. 8, and then appears in first inversion. Frequent shifting and delaying of accents reinforce this tonal ambiguity and make basic metrical patterns obscure. This effect is prominent in "Warum?" the second episode of "Grillen," and the close of "Ende vom Lied."

Each piece has its own distinct expressive character. "Warum?" maintains its spirit of revery throughout, while "In der Nacht," a passionate nocturne (note use of the *passionato* key, ƒ) with a contrasting midsection, possesses an intensity not usually associated with Schumann. "Grillen," mostly in major, is jovial. The last piece, "Ende vom Lied," is in the character of a march. Its extraordinary coda clearly demonstrates the Romantic preoccupation with sonority and color, here manifested by sonorous chords primarily in the bass associated with nonfunctional, coloristic chord progressions from among which, as a dream-like reflection at the conclusion of the piece, the beginning of its main theme appears in augmentation.

---

   [1] In other anthologies: Excerpts from *Carnaval* are in CMS (extensive) and MSO (two); *Papillons* is complete in *AMA*, which also has excerpts from *Album für die Jugend*. Samples of his prose appear in MA 18–9, *MWW*, and *SRMH*.

SCHUMANN: *Phantasiestücke,* "Warum?" (op. 12, no. 3)

SCHUMANN: *Phantasiestücke,* "Grillen" (op. 12, no. 4)

SCHUMANN: *Phantasiestücke,* "In der Nacht" (op. 12. no. 5)

SCHUMANN: *Phantasiestücke,* "Ende vom Lied" (op. 12, no. 8)

*) Dieses poco ritardando ist nur als eine Anregung aufzufassen den Auftakt in reizvoller Weise zu behandeln
This poco ritardando is to be regarded as merely a suggestion for giving added charm to the up-beat
Ce poco ritardando ne doit être considéré qu'à titre d'indication; il faut jouer avec charme la mesure préliminaire

Songs

   A. "Widmung" from *Myrthen* (op. 25, no. 1)
   B. "Zwielicht" from *Liederkreis* (op. 39, no. 10)

In 1840 Schumann turned to the composition of *Lieder*, a genre he previously had deprecated, completing over 200 in that year alone. Previously, Schumann's conversion to *Lieder* has been attributed to his engagement and marriage to Clara Wieck. More recent interpretations emphasize his belief at the time that he had exhausted the possibilities of instrumental music, as well as the fact that song collections were more profitable in the market of the time than was piano music.[1]

    Our first song, "Widmung" ("Dedication"), opens the collection called *Myrthen* (*Myrtles*, op. 25). Set to a poem by Rückert, it is a warm, lyrical expression of love. It is cast in three-part form, with the midsection incorporating material from the first part, and concludes with an extended postlude. The elaborations in the setting relate mostly to rhythm, particularly through the exploitation of the ambiguities inherent in 3/2 meter, along with the frequent accentuation of the third beat. With respect to harmony, note the enharmonic switch A♭ = G♯, which makes possible the move to the distant key of E for the midsection.

    "Zwielicht" ("Twilight"), from the *Liederkreis* (*Circle of Songs*, op. 39), devoted to settings of poems by Eichendorff,[2] creates the completely different mood of distrust in a bleak atmosphere of foreboding and mystery (the poem originally appeared in Eichendorff's novel *Ahnung und Gegenwart*). Schumann expressed this with a winding chromatic line in which the tritone is prominent—here, as usual, symbolic of evil—and by avoiding the tonic (*e*), particularly in the vocal part. Moreover, the song, most unusually, has a contrapuntal accompaniment. Up to the last strophe the upper part of the accompaniment is largely doubled by the vocal line. The music reinforces the strophic form of the poem, although there are changes in detail from strophe to strophe, as in the last strophe, where the counterpoint is dropped in favor of homophony for the warning and conclusion.

TRANSLATIONS

A. DEDICATION

Strophe 1

   You are my soul, my heart,
   my joy, my pain,
   you are the world in which I live,
   the heaven through which I fly,
   the grove to which I commit all my
     sorrow.

Strophe 2

   You are my quiet, my peace,
   you have been sent me from heaven;
   your love makes me worthy,
   your glance transfigures me;
   loving you makes me rise above
     myself,
   you are my good spirit, my better
     self!

---

[1] See L. Plantinga, *Schumann as Critic* (New Haven: Yale, 1967), 179 ff., and B. Turchin, "Schumann's Conversion to Vocal Music," *MQ*, 67 (1981): 392.

[2] The nocturnal song "Mondnacht" from the same set is reprinted in *MSO* and *NSe*. Excerpts from the song cycle *Frauenliebe und Leben* are in *CSM*, and the complete *Dichterliebe* is in *NCS*.

Strophe 3

>You are my soul, my heart,
>my joy, my pain;
>you are the world in which I live,
>the heaven through which I fly,
>my good spirit, my better self.

B. TWILIGHT

Strophe 1

>Evening starts to spread its wings,
>the trees rustle fearfully,
>clouds pass by like somber dreams—
>what does all this mean?

Strophe 2

>If you love one doe more than
>   others,

do not let her graze alone;
there are hunters in the woods;
they sound their horns here and
     move on.

Strophe 3

>If you have a friend here,
>do not trust him at this moment;
>though he may seem friendly,
>yet this is deceit—he plans war.

Strophe 4

>What today goes to bed exhausted
>will rise tomorrow as if born anew;
>much gets lost at night—
>stay on guard—awake and alert.

SCHUMANN: *Myrthen,* "Widmung" (op. 25, no. 1)

SCHUMANN: *Liederkreis,* "Zwielicht" (op. 39, no. 10)

Piano Quintet in E♭ (op. 44)

Generally regarded as the foremost product of Schumann's involvement with chamber music in 1842, this quintet was completed in a mere six days in the fall and published the following year. As a genre, the piano quintet had not had a long history; the most prominent examples were by Mozart, Beethoven, and Schubert, although the scorings vary somewhat (Mozart and Beethoven wrote for piano and winds, Schubert for piano and a special ensemble of strings). But Schumann's combination of piano with string quartet had been anticipated by both Boccherini and Prince Louis Ferdinand of Prussia.

As the century progressed, the genres of chamber music without piano (string quartet and quintet) lost their prominence to those with piano, where the part writing could be less rigorous. This trend is clear in the work of Schumann, who wrote but three works of chamber music without piano—the three string quartets (op. 41). On the other hand, Schumann consistently used the large four-movement form of the older string quartet and symphony, as in this composition. Its four movements include an Allegro in E♭ in sonata form, a March in c, a Scherzo in E♭ with two contrasting trios, and a complex concluding Allegro in the main key (see the outline that follows). Thus the form of the work as a whole and the forms of its individual movements are on the whole traditional. Symbolic of this is the retention of the double bar with repeat marks at the end of the exposition in the first movement. The only pronouncedly Romantic structural aspect involves explicit cyclic form: the reappearance of the first movement's principal theme as the culmination of the finale.

The piano provides support for solo passages in individual string instruments, as in the secondary theme and development of the first movement or the first trio of the Scherzo. Alternatively, the piano frequently opposes the strings in concerto-like fashion. This relationship to the concerto is underlined by occasional virtuoso writing in the piano part, mostly octave passages, again in the development of the first movement, but also in the second episode of the second, and the Scherzo proper.

An interesting and unexpected feature is the similarity of the second movement to its counterpart in Beethoven's *Eroica* Symphony.[1] Not only are both movements funeral marches (explicitly in the Symphony, implicitly in the Quintet), but the episodes are in the same keys, C and f. Moreover, in both, the character of the second episode is carried on into the recapitulation. There are, however, some differences. Schumann has his recapitulation in f, returning to the tonic only at the end of the movement; also, unlike Beethoven, he strictly follows the scheme of the conventional rondo, repeating the first episode.

The Quintet also displays the characteristically Romantic emphasis on melody and color. Most of the themes are set in a lyric fashion, an especially good example being the first episode of the second movement. Probably the best instance of a special sonority may be found in the first, second, and last presentations of the march in the second movement. The effect is achieved through the use of the middle and low registers, the voices in close position, pizzicato in the accompanying strings, regular

---

[1] See MCP, No. 26.

and fairly quick harmonic rhythm, usually two chords to a bar, and a relative weakening of the tonic by emphasis on the subdominant and submediant. On its third presentation, however, the march is radically transformed. It maintains the *agitato* of the second episode and incorporates the main motive from that episode in violin I and cello, with the main theme in the viola, tremolo in violin II, and broken chords in triple rhythm in the piano.

The form of the finale is ambivalent, and has been construed in two ways—as a sonata-rondo or as an altered and elaborated version of the sonata structure. The following outline shows these two interpretations:

As Sonata-rondo	Thematic/Functional Elements[1]	Bar Numbers	As Sonata Form[2]
Rondo	P, c–Eb	1	Exposition
	T	43	
Episode I	1S, E	114	Development
	P, c#	136	
Rondo (development)	P, Eb	164	Recapitulation
	T	178	
Episode II	2S, Bb	224	Exposition II
Rondo	P, c–Eb, fugal	248	Development II
Episode I	1S, Eb–Ab	274	
Rondo	P, Eb, fugal with theme from I	319	
Episode II	2S, Eb	378	Recapitulation II
Coda/Rondo	K>P, Eb	402	Coda

[1] Symbols from J. LaRue, *Guidelines for Style Analysis* (New York: Norton, 1970), 153 ff.: P=principal or primary theme; S=secondary theme; T=transition; K=concluding theme.
[2] See H. Ulrich, *Chamber Music*, 2nd ed. (New York: Columbia, 1966), 292.

SCHUMANN: Piano Quintet in E♭ (op. 44)

189

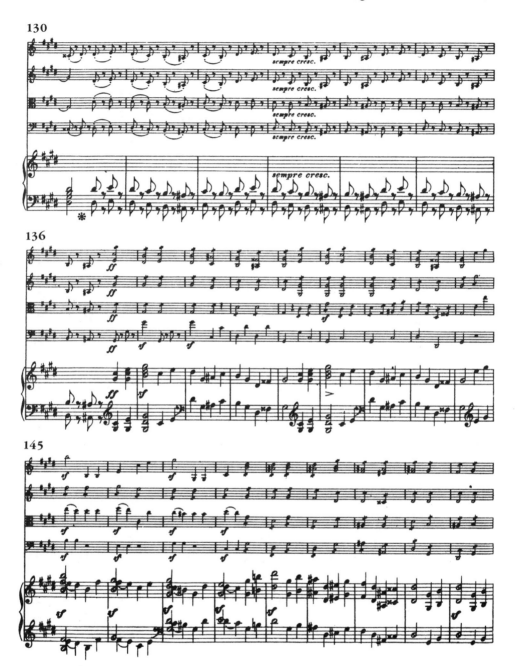

The Early Phase in France and Italy

Romanticism in music took on different forms in France and Italy. In France, the Romantic impetus clearly came mostly from Germany, as is clear from Mme. de Staël's influential book *De l'Allemagne* (1810), with its indebtedness to the ideas of the Schlegels, who were leading figures in the German Romantic literary movement. But France, after all, had been a center of European culture, had undergone the most violent and influential revolution of the time, and had produced Rousseau, an early apostle of the doctrine of subjective expression. The new works of art, literature, and music created in France exhibited a magnificence of size and scope, a preoccupation with heroic themes, grand gestures, and emphatic expression totally unlike anything in Germany. It is, that is to say, a large step from Tieck, Brentano, and Eichendorff to Stendal and Hugo, from Caspar David Friedrich to Delacroix, and from Schubert to Berlioz, even though the basic suppositions are the same. Moreover, despite the early appearance of Rousseau and the work of Chateaubriand and Mme. de Staël, Romanticism did not become a movement in France until the 1820s.

In Italy, on the other hand, opera remained the leading preoccupation of musicians, so that the mainstream of Germanically-oriented Romanticism had relatively little effect here.[1] More and more the newer Italian operas came to be based on the work of English, German, and French writers, whose influence was reflected in the new emphasis on sudden twists of plot, violent confrontations, and lurid contrasts—none of which are characteristic of eighteenth-century *opera seria*. Musically, a loosening of the traditional forms can be noted, even though older conventions maintained their importance as well.

The leading French musician of the period was Hector Berlioz (1803–1869), a composer, conductor, and writer, as well as librarian. He composed a number of works with literary associations, mostly orchestral, which demonstrate his interest in unusual—and, at the time, unprecedented—sonorities and in expression on a grand scale. Frédéric Chopin (1810–1849), while born and trained in Poland, spent his mature life in Paris. In contrast to Berlioz, Chopin neglected the orchestra, devoting himself almost exclusively to the piano.

---

[1] See the contemporary assessment of the situation in Italy in *MWW*, No. 100.

Section One: Berlioz

"Roméo seul—Tristesse—Bruits lointains de Concert du bal—Grande fête chez Capulet," from *Roméo et Juliette* (op. 17), Part Two

Although Berlioz emphasized the concert overture early in his career as a composer, he also worked with the symphony, which he adapted to an extramusical content—a program, as it is usually called—usually of a literary nature. There are three principal works: the *Symphonie fantastique* in C (op. 14) of 1830 (revised 1831);[1] *Harold en Italie* in g-G (op. 16) of 1834, originally written for Paganini; and *Roméo et Juliette* in b-B of 1839. Berlioz himself provided the program for the first, which explores the fantasies of an artist who, unhappy in love, has resorted to drugs. The sources of the other two were Byron's *Childe Harold's Pilgrimage* and Shakespeare's play. The relationship of the first two to the traditional symphonic form seems clear enough, with the principal departure being the use of a recurring musical theme specifically associated with an aspect of the program: the *idée fixe* in the former, Harold's theme in the latter. Thus both are cyclic compositions. Because they are based on extramusical material, these compositions are known as *program symphonies*.

The relation to the conventional symphony is less clear in *Roméo et Juliette*, adapted from Shakespeare by Emile Deschamps. Unlike the earlier works, *Roméo et Juliette* has vocal elements, solo and choral, and makes use of operatic styles, thereby justifying Berlioz's own description of it as a *symphonie dramatique*. The symphony consists of six movements and is organized in three parts. Some sections feature singing, while others are purely instrumental. This arrangement obviously does not square with any ordinary notion of a symphony, but the example of Beethoven's Symphony 9 was influential. Even so, an examination of the purely instrumental movements reveals many similarities to a symphony (Roman numbers indicate traditional movements of a symphony; Arabic numbers refer to Berlioz's own enumeration of the sections):

---

[1] Reprinted complete in S and NCS; the latter, ed. by E. Cone (1971), has excellent historical and analytical material; the fourth movement is in NSe, the fifth in MSO. Examples of Berlioz's prose are in MA 18-9, MWW, and SRMH.

PART ONE	PART TWO			PART THREE	
	I	II	III	IV	V
1. Introduction (Overture), b (orchestra) 2. Prologue, a Recitative and aria elements Overview of plot (soloists, chorus, orchestra)	1. Andante & Allegro, C–F Romeo alone— Sadness— Festival at Capulets (orchestra)	2. Introduction (vocal) Adagio, A Love scene (orchestra)	3. Scherzo, F Queen Mab (orchestra)	1. Funeral March, a–E (chorus and orchestra) 2. Romeo in the Tomb of the Capulets, e–A (orchestra)	3. Finale Sectional ensemble, a–B (soloists, chorus, orchestra)

Thus the work can be thought of as a five-movement symphony, with a finale in two separate parts, to which an introduction has been added. The Adagio and Scherzo would be the most traditional movements in this context. The vocal passages and operatic elements appear mostly in the Introduction and Finale, which frame four largely instrumental movements. As a whole the symphony is tonally closed, even though the movement discussed here is not. Berlioz abandoned the standard use of sonata structure in the first movement as well as the use of a cyclic theme; however, themes with definite associations recur in more than one movement, and these are anticipated in the Prologue.

Despite his inclusion of vocal music, Berlioz shared the Romantic view of the ultimate power of pure instrumental music to express emotions. Indeed the most crucial parts of the symphony are purely instrumental. In his preface to the love and tomb scenes Berlioz explained "the sublimity of love made its expression so full of danger for the composer, that he preferred to give a wider latitude to his imagination than would have been possible with words. He had recourse to the instrumental medium, a richer, more varied, less limited language, and by its very vagueness infinitely more powerful."[2]

The "first movement" of the work[3] is cast in an unusual—indeed unprecedented—form. The composer's characteristic use of thematic transformation can be seen throughout the movement. This particularly involves the "C" theme (see the outline, which follows), which is later combined with the "festival" theme ("D"). This essentially operatic device is common in his work.[4] The felicitous touches of scoring include pizzicato, combinations of winds and strings, and brass, harp, triangle, tambourines, sponge-tipped mallets for the timpani, and the long oboe solo. The extravagant character of the movement is typical of French Romanticism.

The following outline attempts to do justice to the loose organization of the movement:

---

[2] In the preface to the score; quoted by J. Barzun, *Berlioz and the Romantic Century*, i (Boston: Little, Brown, 1950), 322.

[3] The Queen Mab Scherzo is reprinted in *NAWM*, the beginning of the work in *CSM* (piano reduction).

[4] See J. Langford, "The Dramatic Symphony of Berlioz as an Outgrowth of the French Operatic Tradition," *MQ* 69 (1983): 85.

Tempo/Character Marking and Key	Bar Number	Thematic/Formal Elements[1]	Plot	Character/Style and Remarks

Andante malinconico, C	1	A a
		   b
		   c
		   d
			Romeo alone	Lyric: arioso, chromatic; solo lines; note motive (a^x), b. 8–9 and 15–16

Allegro, C	63	B>a^x	Distant sounds of dance orchestra [which accompany]	Lyric, fast; note sponge-tipped mallets and tambourines
Larghetto espressivo, C	81	C	Sadness	Aria, oboe has melody punctuated with rhythm from B
Allegro, F	107	1T		

——	128	D>a^x
		  e
		  d
			Grand festival at Capulets	Exuberant dance

	206	E		
——	225	C & D		"Réunion des deux thèmes"; use of harps
	266	2T		
	278	B>a^x		Quasi-fugue over 4-bar descending ostinato; then crescendo with motive from B and D
——	298	F		With ostinato from preceding passage
	332	G		Figuration (repeated once, then varied)
Tempo I, F	396	Coda		Note recall of C

[1] Capital letters indicate sections, lowercase letters subsections; the superscript "x" indicates the important motive; T stands for a transition, of which there are two here; > means "derived from."

BERLIOZ: *Roméo et Juliette*, Part Two, Roméo seul—Tristesse—Bruits lointains de Concert du bal—Grande fête chez Capulet (op. 17)

119

Baguettes d'éponge. *Schwammschlägel.* Sponge-headed drum-sticks.

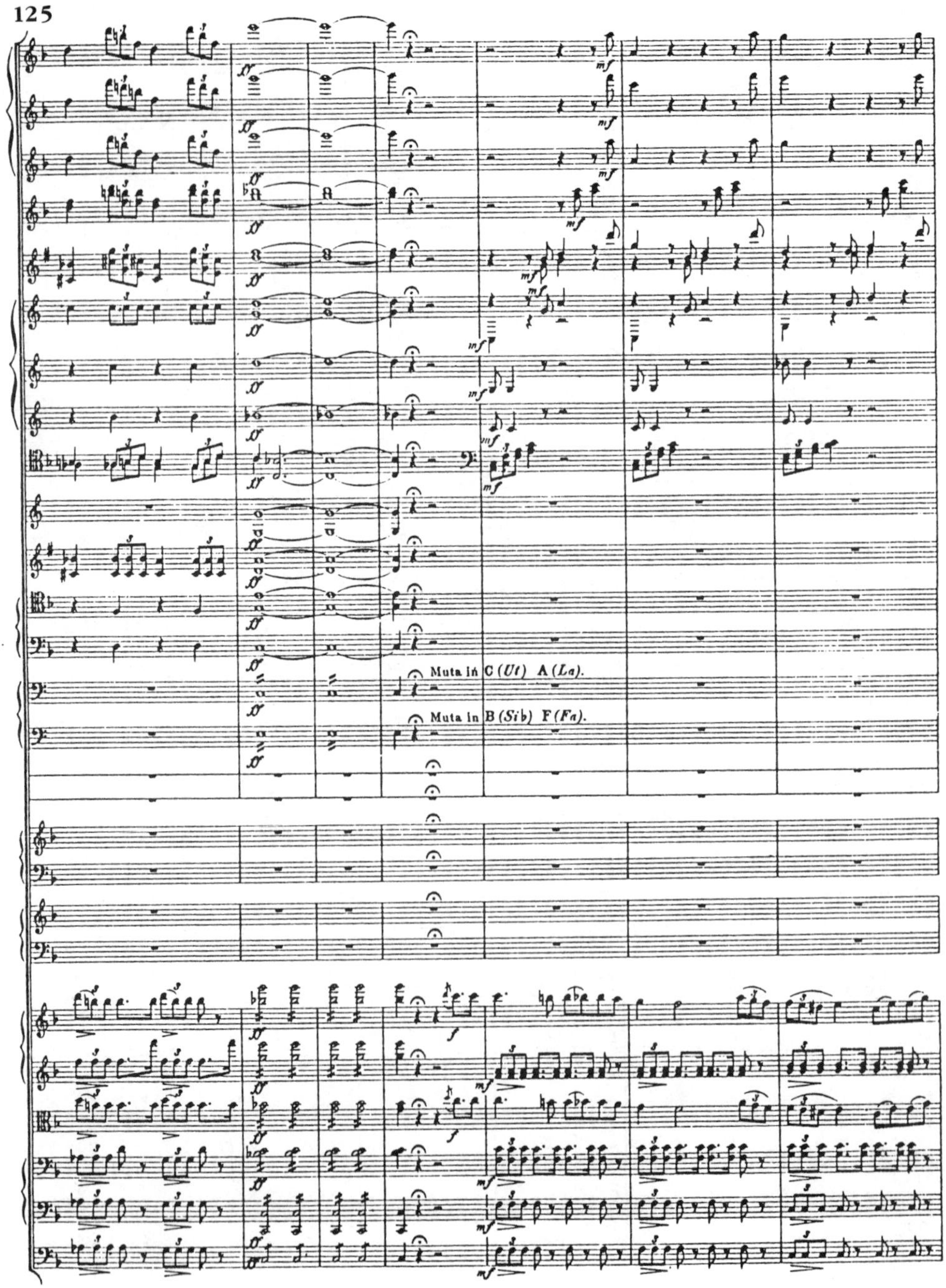
125
Muta in C (Ut) A (La).
Muta in B (Sib) F (Fa).

132

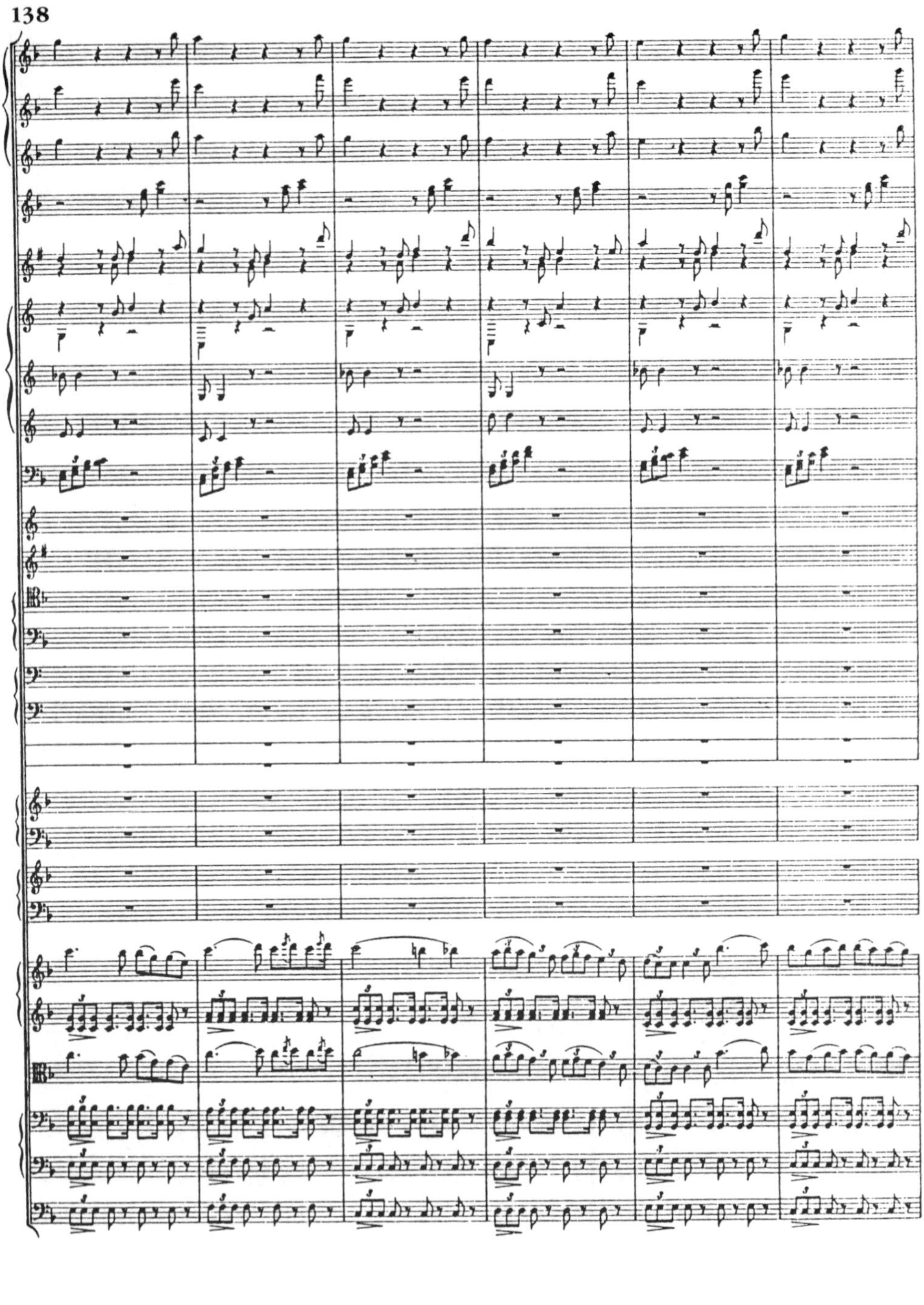

144

156

162

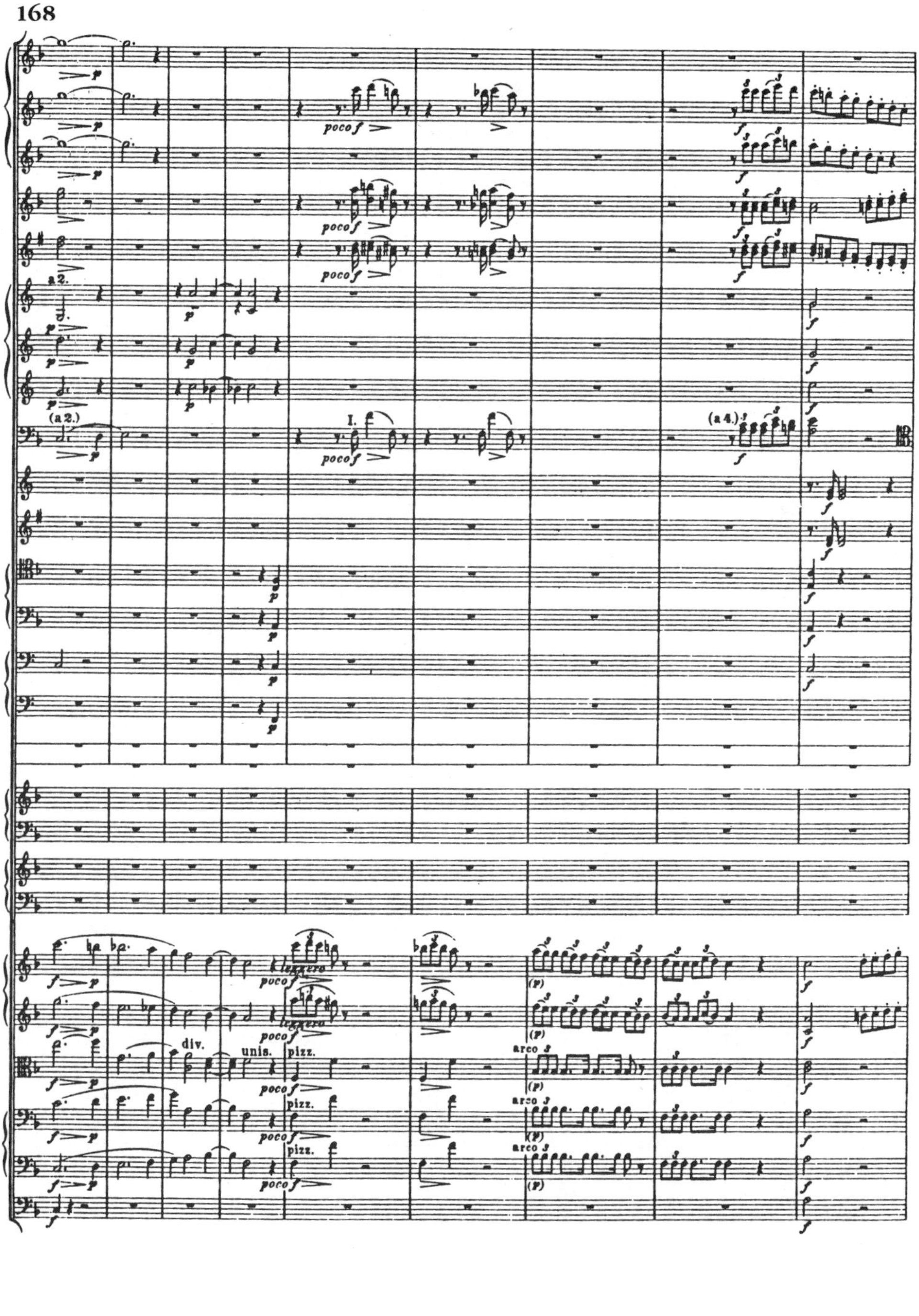
168
a 2.
(a 2.)
poco f
I.
(a 4.)
div.
unis.
pizz.
leggiero
arco

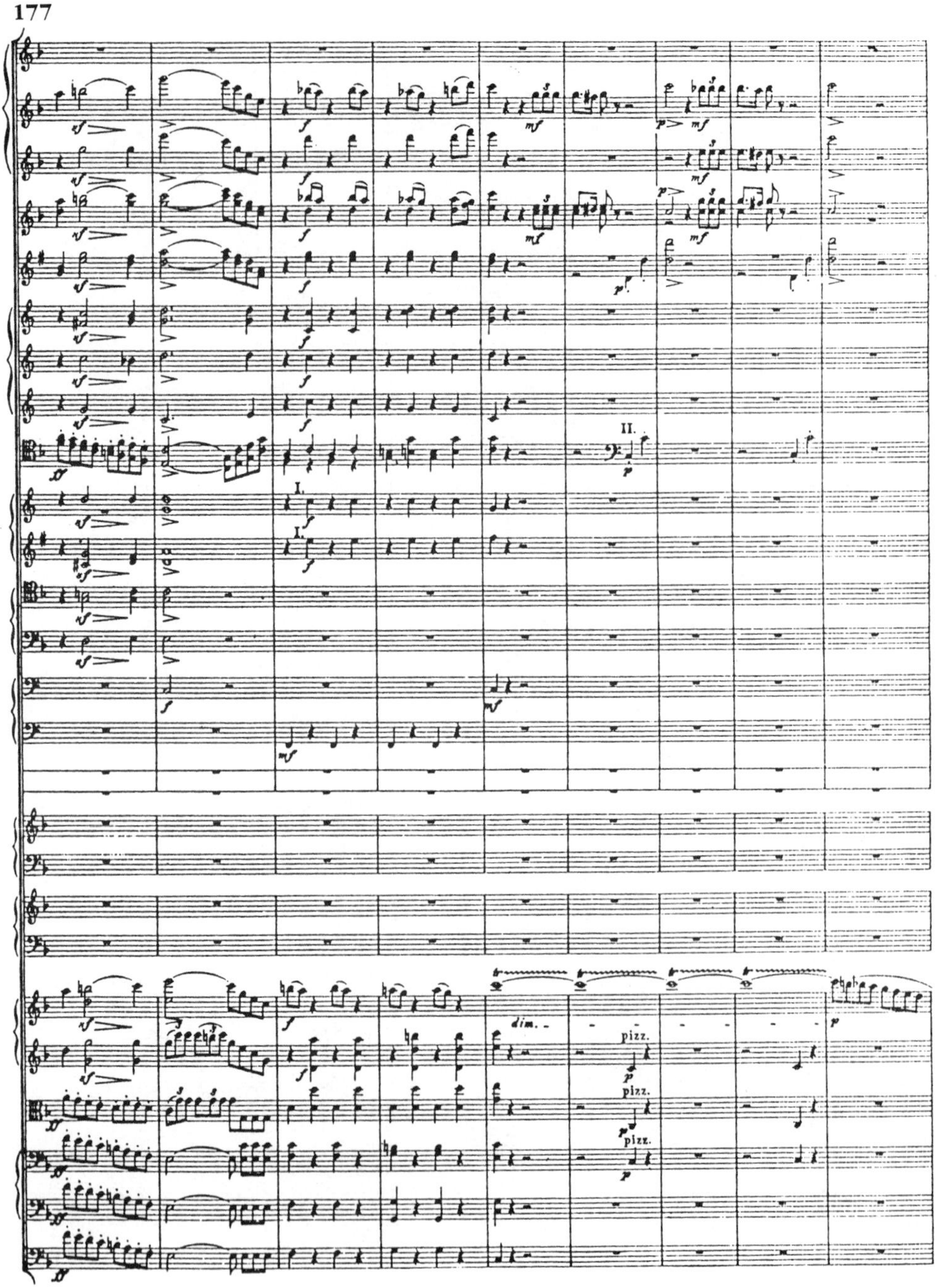
177
II.
I.
I.
dim.
pizz.
pizz.
pizz.

186

193

200

207

215

223

Réunion des deux Thèmes, du Larghetto et de l'Allegro.
Vereinigung der zwei Themen, des Larghetto und des Allegro.
The two themes, Larghetto and Allegro combined.

231

238

245

252

259

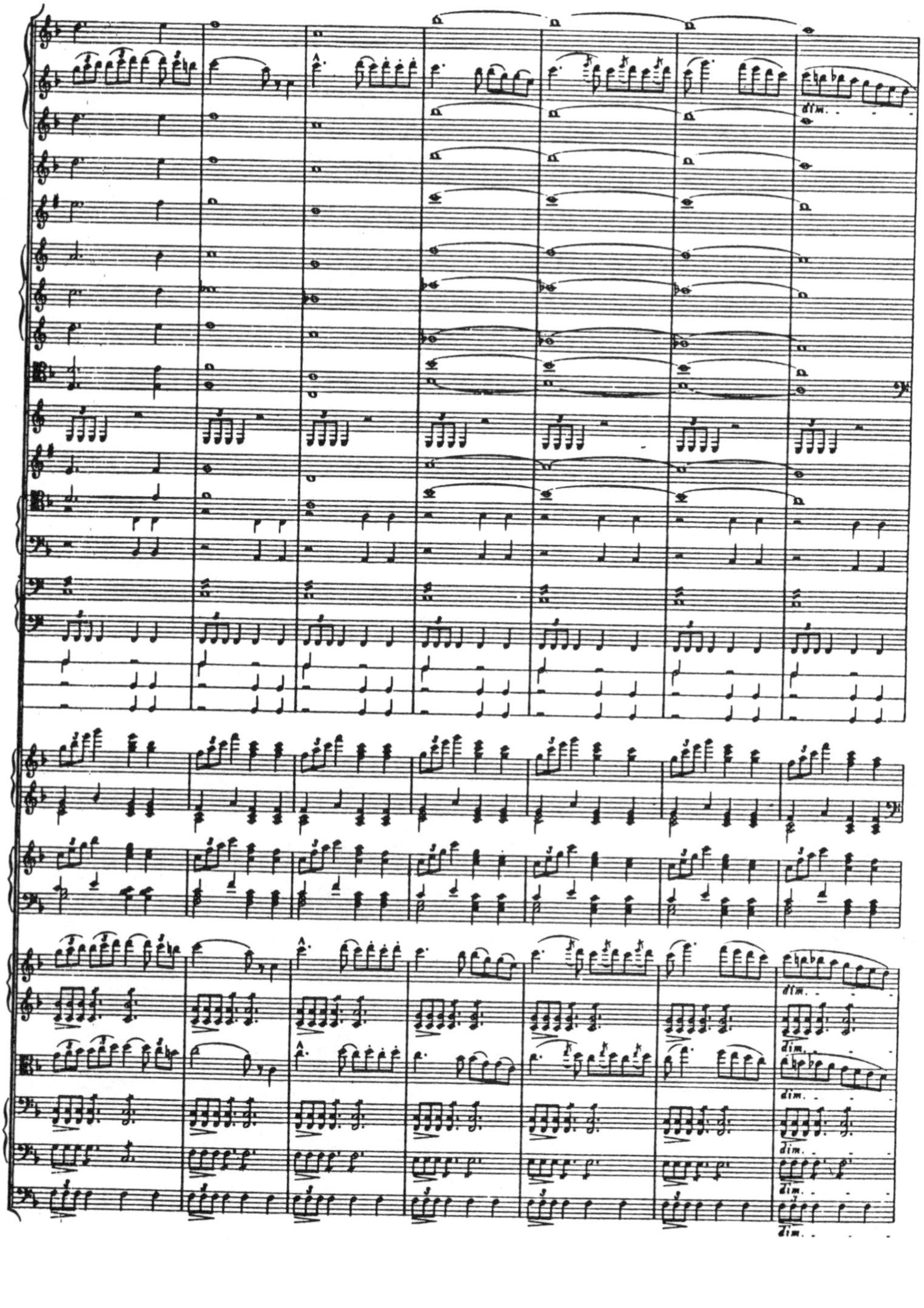

266

274

senza accelerando

senza accelerando

286

320

328

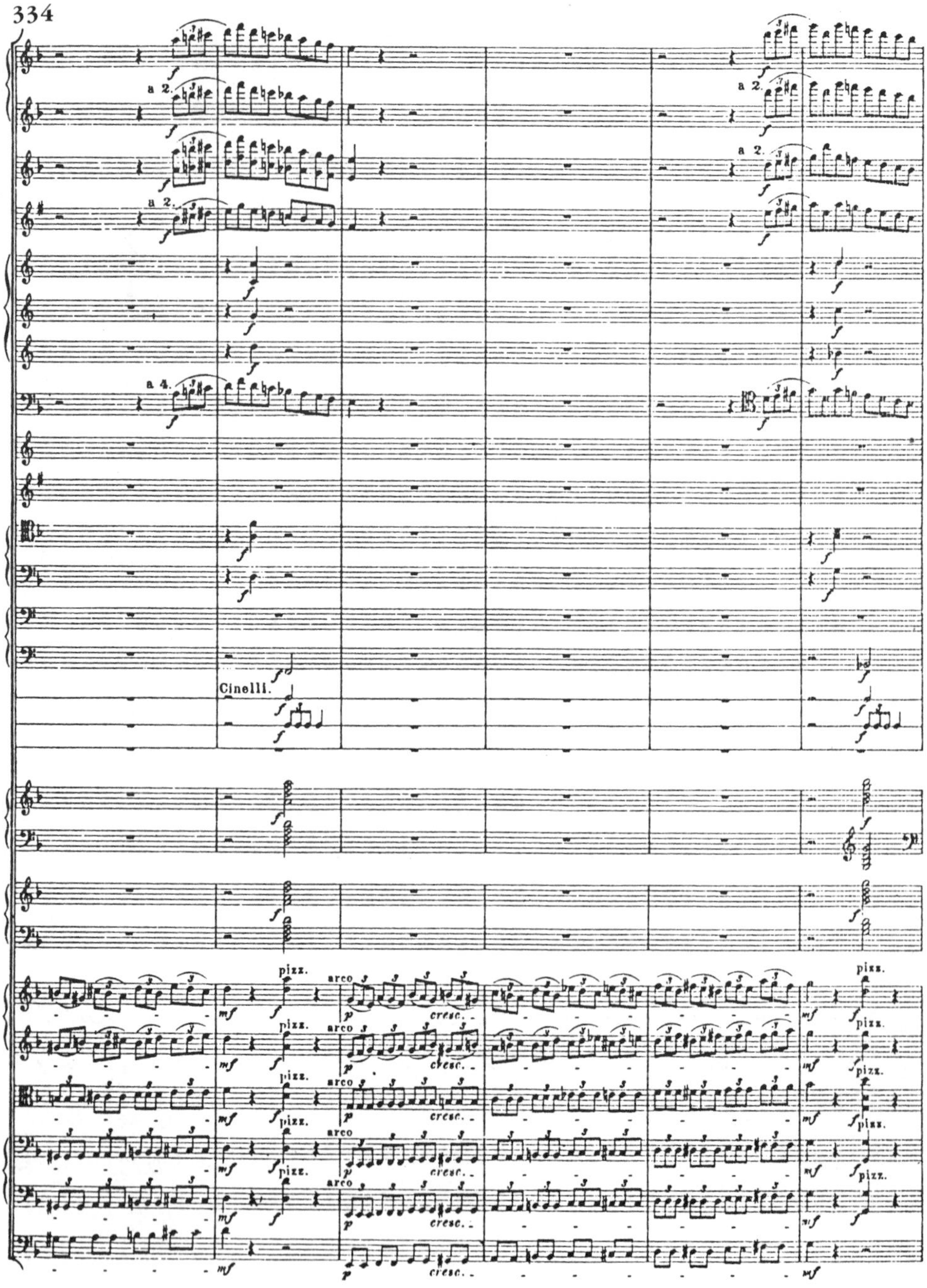
334
a 2.
a 4.
Cinelli.
pizz.
arco
cresc.
mf
f
p

340
a 2
a 2
arco
cresc. molto
arco
cresc. molto
arco
cresc. molto
arco
cresc. molto
arco
cresc. molto
cresc. molto

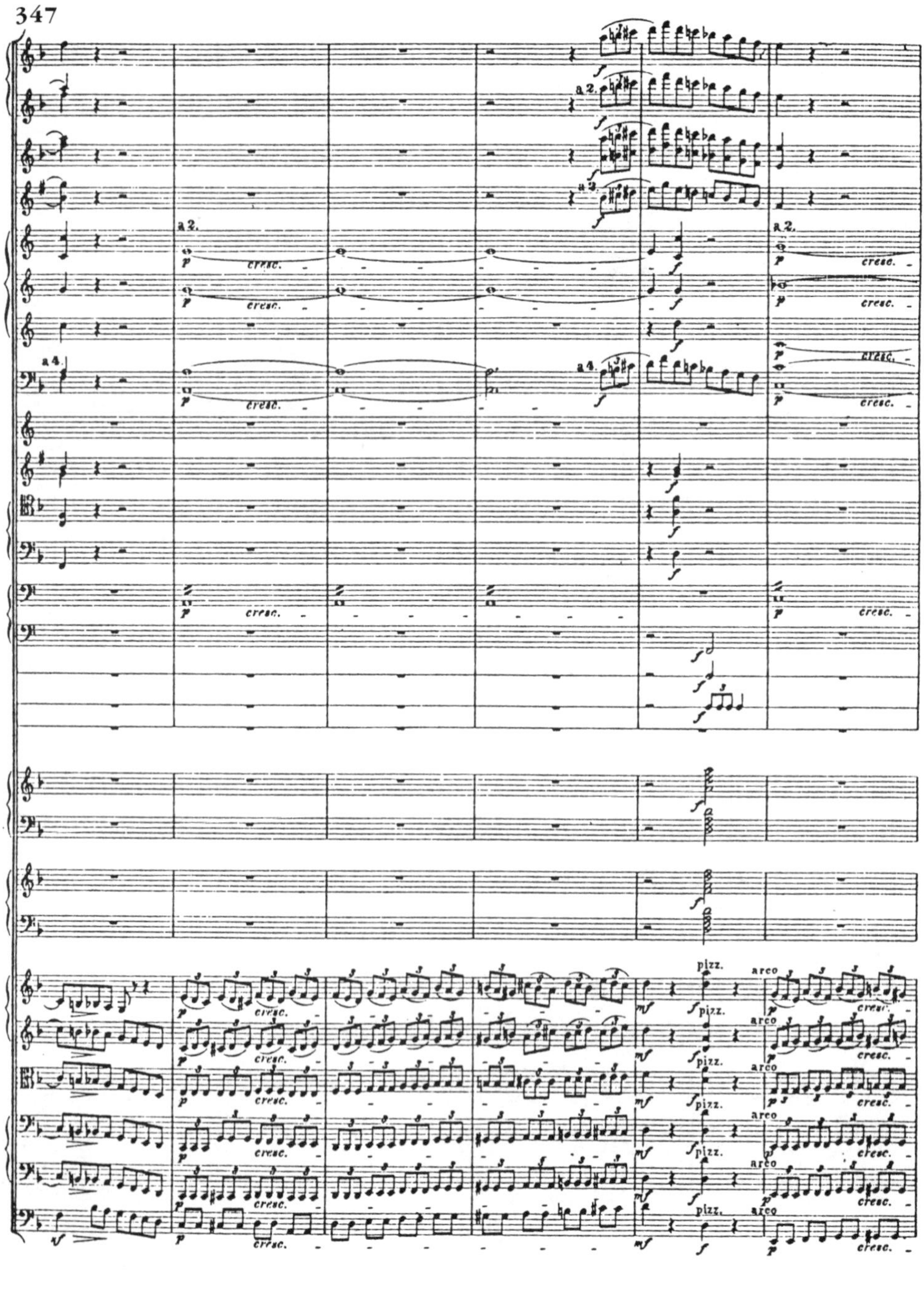
347
a 2.
a 4.
cresc.
pizz.
arco

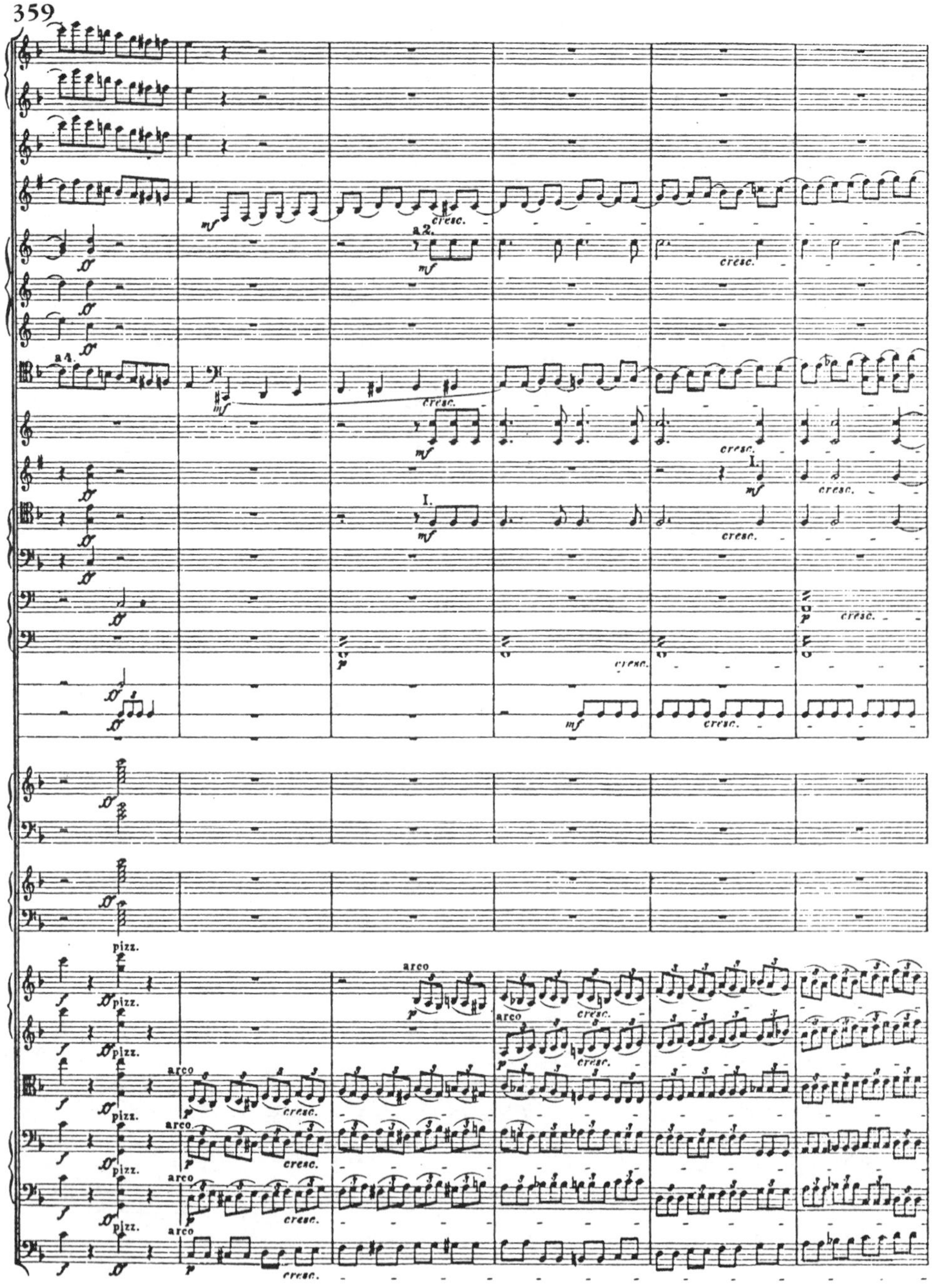
359
a 4.
a 2.
I.
I.
cresc.
pizz.
arco

365

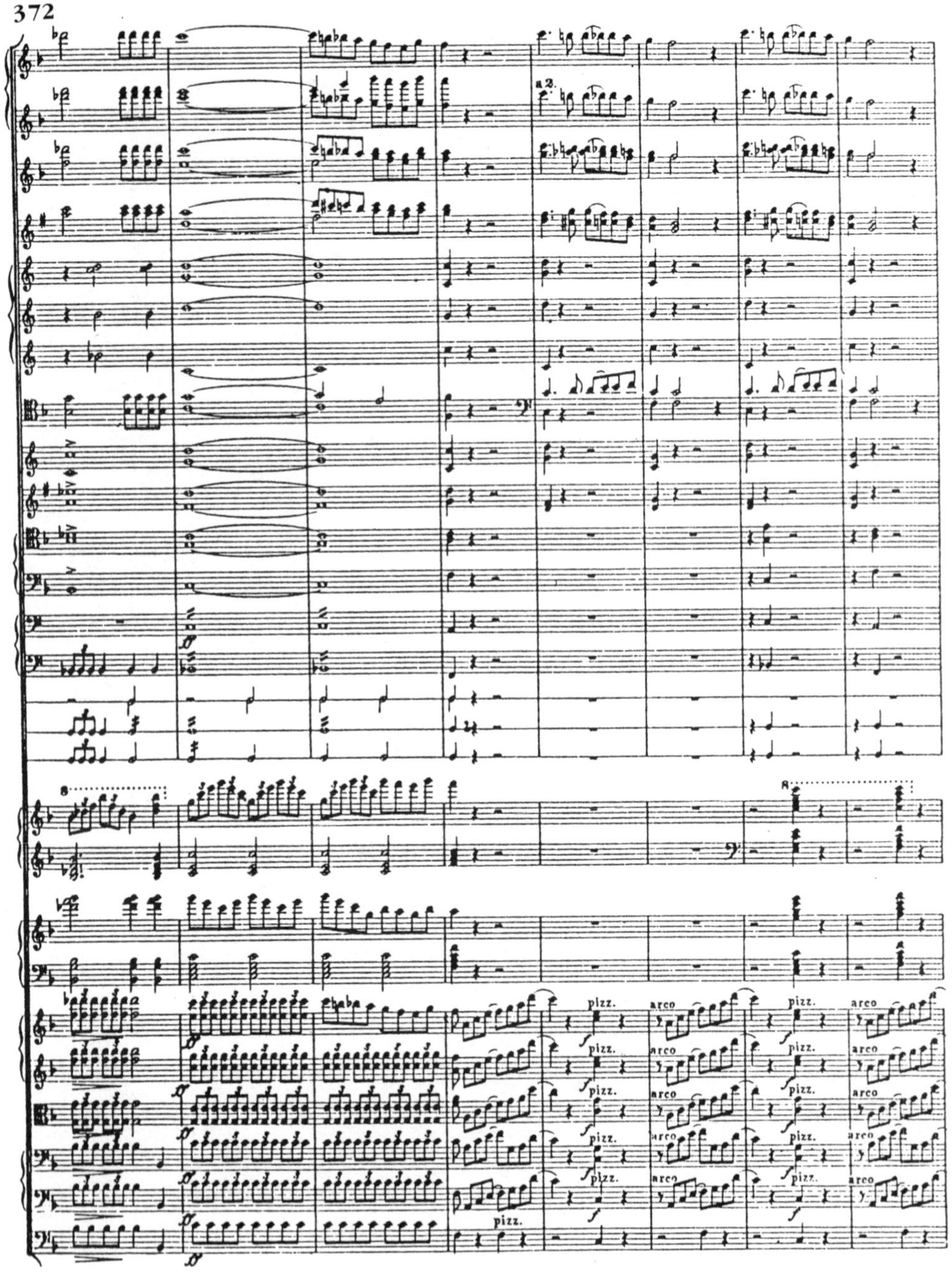
372
a2.
pizz.
arco

380

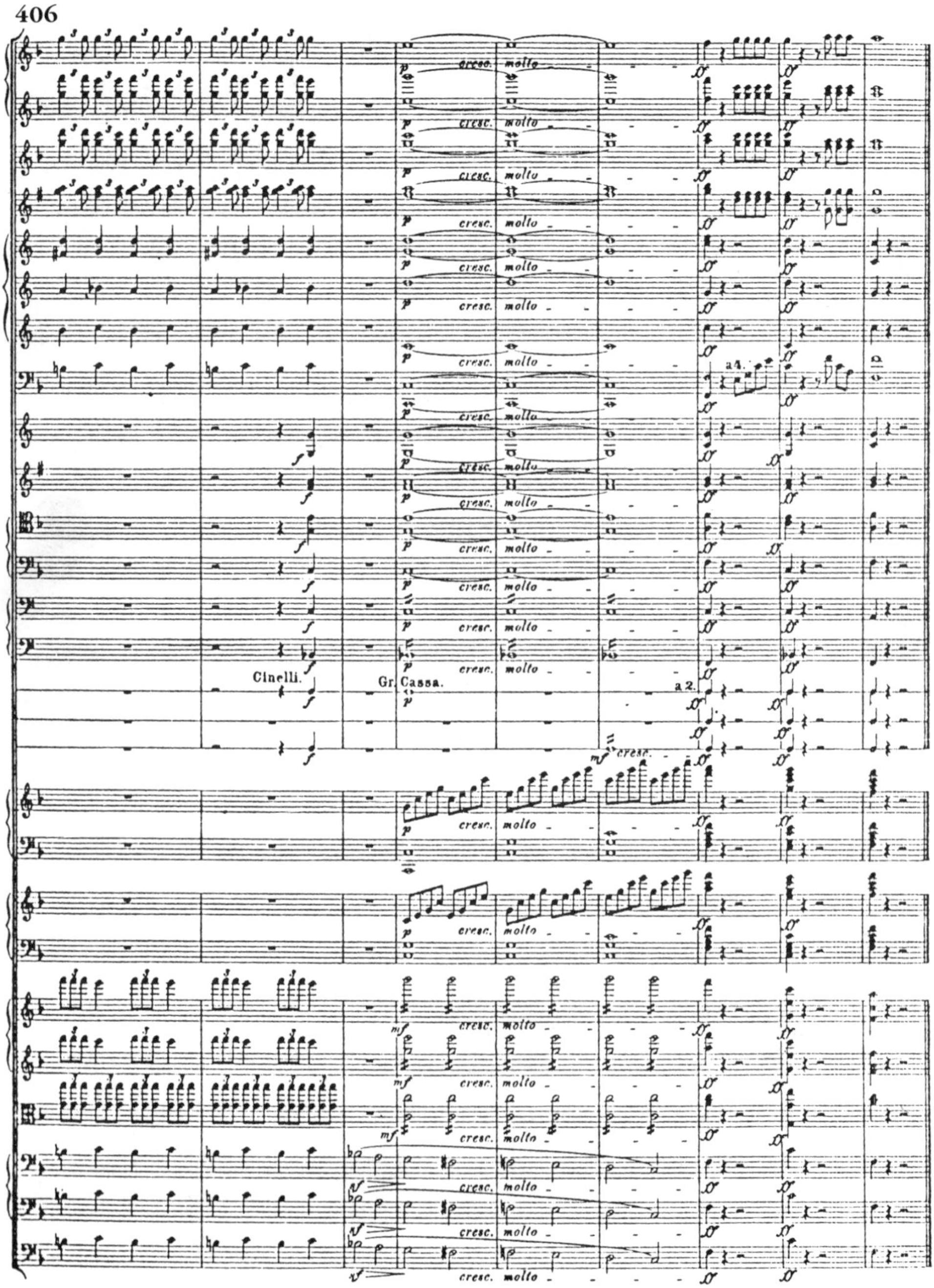
406
cresc.
molto
a 4.
Cinelli.
Gr. Cassa.
a 2.

Section Two: Chopin

Mazurkas (B. 77/op. 17)[1]
A. Vivo e risoluto in B♭ (no. 1)
B. Lento ma non troppo in e (no. 2)

The word *mazurka* is considered to be the gallicized version of *mazur* or *mazurek*, the name given to circle dances for couples native to the plain of Mazovia, near Warsaw. These dances feature triple meter, with the accent frequently on the second beat and the first beat often subdivided. Chopin also included other Polish dance-types among his mazurkas, such as the fast *obertas* and the slow *kujawiak*, the latter often in the minor; frequently these were combined in a single piece. Of the two mazurkas discussed here, however, the first is mostly an *obertas*, the second a *kujawiak*.[2] They were composed in 1832–1833 and published in 1834.

Both pieces follow the traditional three-part formal scheme; the first a true Da Capo, the second with coda. Chopin's harmony is characterized by frequent seventh chords, here particularly on accented beats. His melodies emphasize nonharmonic—and frequently dissonant—tones, as is clear from the second of the two mazurkas. Note in the first mazurka the reharmonization of certain passages in their restatement, as in the "a" phrase of the principal theme (compare b. 3 with b. 19). In both midsections (the term "trio" is not used) the drone bass suggests the *duda* (bagpipe), an instrument commonly used for such dances. The dissonances in the midsection of the first mazurka are produced in part by the use of both the normal and flat forms of the main degrees of the scale: tonic, fourth, fifth (the section is in E♭). Such a passage provoked the ire of the conservative critic Ludwig Rellstab, who in reference to the mazurkas spoke of their "odd originality," "unnatural positions," "ear-splitting dischords, forced transitions, harsh modulations, ugly distortions of melody and rhythm."[3]

Chopin's music has presented problems for his editors. Discrepancies between manuscripts and first editions often make it difficult to discern his actual intentions.[4] At issue are such matters as placement of slurs, kinds of articulation signs, direction of stems, and so on. The edition of the mazurkas reproduced here follows the text of the first French edition (Paris, M. Schlesinger, 1834).

---

[1] The "B" numbers come from M. J. E. Brown, *Chopin: An Index to his Works in Chronological Order* (London: Macmillan, 1960; 2nd ed., 1972). See also K. Kobylánska, *Frédéric Chopin: Thematisch-bibliographisches Werkverzeichnis*, trans. H. Stolze (Munich-Duisburg: Henle, 1979).

[2] See A. Harasowski, "An Overview of Chopin's Piano Music," *PQ* 113 (29th Year, Spring 1981): 18 and 22. For another *kujawiak*, see CSM. Other character pieces by Chopin are in AMA (mazurkas and preludes), CSM, MSO, and NSe. The Piano Concerto 2, *f*, is in C.

[3] Quoted by F. Niecks, *Chopin as Man and Musician*, i (London: Novello, 1890/R New York: Cooper Square, 1973), 269–70.

[4] See T. Higgins, "Whose Chopin?" *19th Century Music* 5 (1981): 67.

CHOPIN: Mazurka in B♭ (B. 77/op. 17, no. 1)

CHOPIN: Mazurka in *e* (B. 77/op. 17, no. 2)

Nocturne, Larghetto in F♯ (B. 55/op. 15, no. 2)

Chopin's more than 20 nocturnes were composed from 1830, the year he left Warsaw, until the end of his career. He took over the genre as it had been established by the Irish pianist and composer John Field, but through many enrichments, chiefly harmonic, he made it over into something completely his own.[1] The Larghetto in F♯, composed in 1830–1831 and published, together with two other nocturnes, in 1834, is an excellent example of the genre.

The formal scheme is ternary, with a short transition between the main and midsections, and a coda. The midsection, to be played twice as fast, provides contrast, its melodic line animated by dotted rhythms. This leads to the climax of the piece, and a restatement of the first section follows. In the coda there is a good example of the Romantic preoccupation with sonority: Delicate triadic figuration, beginning very high, descends gradually in sequences over the standard accompanimental pattern, all in tonic harmony.

The melodic line is for the most part organized in phrases eight bars in length, accompanied by a standard pattern of figuration and ornamented with trills and grace notes. Figuration is important in the melodic line as well. In b. 11 the melody itself "dissolves," as it were, into a chain of grace notes in a passage doubtless to be played very much in tempo rubato. Thus Chopin's nocturnes in general resemble arias in the Italian opera of the time (see Bellini, "Me Chiami, o Norma," later in this chapter). Numerous expression marks indicate the various moods evoked in the first section. Note throughout the use of the pedal.

Rellstab was particularly venemous with respect to the nocturnes, especially in regard to harmony: "where Field smiles, Chopin makes a grinning grimace; where Field cries, Chopin groans; where Field puts some seasoning into his food, Chopin empties a whole handful of cayenne pepper."[2]

Again our edition follows the text of the first French edition (Paris, Schlesinger, 1834).

---

[1] See *NAWM*, where a nocturne by Field is followed by one by Chopin. See Liszt's view of Field, *MWW*, No. 105. *AMA* has Chopin's Nocturne in D♭ (B. 96/ op. 27 ii).
[2] Quoted by Niecks, *Chopin as Man and Musician*, i, 269–70.

CHOPIN: Nocturne in F♯ (B. 55/op. 15, no. 2)

Ballade in ƒ (B. 146/op. 52)

For the most part the character piece was conceived as a small form. Chopin, who evidently viewed the smaller form of the character piece as corresponding to lyric poetry, modeled his most important larger character pieces on the ballad, a chief representative of epic (narrative) poetry. His interest in the ballad was probably stimulated by the *Rhapsodies* of Tomášek (the term *rhapsody* frequently connotes much the same thing as ballad) and perhaps by the ballads of his friend the Polish poet Adam Mickiewicz, although no specific correspondences between Chopin's music and Mickiewicz's poetry have been shown.[1] Chopin began work in the genre in 1831 and continued with it until early in the next decade.

The Ballade in ƒ, the fourth and last, was composed in 1842 and published in 1843.[2] Like the other ballades, it is a lengthy piece (about eight minutes), which embodies much contrast of mood and virtuoso display, all in highly chromatic harmony. The association between seriousness and intensity on the one hand and virtuosity on other are reminiscent of Italian opera.

Structurally, this ballade, like the other three, is cast in a form allied to the sonata principle, here with a substantial coda. The form is given a lyrical interpretation, as in the case of the principal theme, which is cast in a traditional scheme ("aaba") with phrase lengths of 7 and 14 bars ("b" incorporates parts of "a"). In the recapitulation the principal theme is submitted to considerable variation.

The Ballade provides another opportunity to note the richness of Chopin's harmonic resources, doubtless the most arresting aspect of his music. His harmony is intensely chromatic, charged with expressive sevenths and ninths, altered chords, chords borrowed from other keys, modulations, nonfunctional progressions, and so on. As noted in connection with the mazurkas, the constant use of nonharmonic—dissonant—tones in the melody, often in conjunction with ornamentation, is characteristic. In the principal theme itself we can note the play between the natural and flat forms of the seventh step, and the melody, moreover, has a way of avoiding cadences on the tonic. On its last statement in the exposition, the "a" is accompanied by a running figuration (b. 56 ff.). The introduction is oriented to the dominant, and the tonic does not arrive until b. 8. Moreover, the secondary theme appears not in A♭ or C, as might be expected, but in B♭.

---

[1] See D. Witten, "Ballads and Ballades," *PQ* 113 (29th Year, Spring 1981); 33.
[2] The Ballade ɪ, g (op. 23) is in MSO.

The Ballade may be outlined as follows:

Section	Bar Number		Theme and Function
Introduction	1	O^1	
Exposition	8	P	element: a a b a
			bar: 8 23 38 58
	71	T	
	84	S	(in Bb; stated twice)
Development or Midsection	100		(Based on P and, later, O; imitation at Retransition)
Recapitulation	139	P	("b" and last statement of "a" are omitted)
	169	S	(extended)
Coda	203		

[1] O = introductory material; P = principal or primary theme; T = transition; S = secondary theme. See LaRue, *Guidelines for Style Analysis,* 154.

Alternatively, the piece could be viewed as an irregular and disproportionate rondo, with P b serving as the first episode and S with the development as the second.

CHOPIN: Ballade in *f* (B. 146/op. 52)

Section Three: Italian and French Opera

Opera, not instrumental music, was supreme in nineteenth-century Italy. Despite the reforms of Gluck and others, in the late eighteenth century the old and magnificent *opera seria* declined in favor of the more modest and deliberately popular *opera buffa*. In the early nineteenth century, however, *opera seria* was revived, but the new operas were on a smaller scale and took their subjects primarily from history and literature rather than from the traditional mythological or quasi-mythological sources.[1]

The application of music to a dramatic text remained fundamentally as it had been: a series of musical numbers connected by recitative; thus the qualification *number opera*. Yet there were some changes. In the *opera seria*, the old *secco* recitative, accompanied only by continuo (often only a harpsichord), gave way to recitative accompanied by the orchestra, while in the *opera buffa* the *secco* tended to be preserved. The newer *parlante* type of recitative became more prominent.[2] As in the last quarter of the eighteenth century, a multiplicity of aria types and a great variety of formal schemes existed. But at the same time a new way of organizing an operatic scene was developed (see Bellini, "Me chiami, o Norma," later in the chapter). Finally, there was a shift toward greater emphasis on ensembles.

The opera examples here come from Gaetano Donizetti (1797–1848), the most representative Italian composer between Rossini and Verdi; and Vincenzo Bellini (1801–1835), who worked with restrained conservatism. The third selection, by Giacomo Meyerbeer (1791–1864), a German who was trained in Italy but had his greatest successes in Paris and later worked in Berlin, represents *grand opera*, an essentially French genre.

---

[1] See F. Lippmann, *Vincenzo Bellini und die italienische Opera Seria seiner Zeit* (Analecta musicologica, vi; Cologne & Vienna: Böhlau, 1969).

[2] See note 4 on p. 11.

Donizetti: "Chi mi frena in tal momento," Recitative and Sextet from *Lucia di Lammermoor*, Act II

Opera seria is well represented among the approximately 60 operas of all styles and types composed by Donizetti. True to the spirit of the time, his *serie* (the term continued to be used in the first half of the nineteenth century) are based on literature and history, and occasionally on the work of major writers such as Byron, Corneille, Dumas, Hugo, Schiller, and Scott. Donizetti's simple and direct approach furthered his goal of being successful with audiences. The plots move swiftly, with quick narrative twists and abundant contrast, far removed from the *opere serie* of the previous century. Correspondingly the musical style features clearly phrased, memorable ("catchy") tunes, frequently organized by short rhythmic patterns.

Lucia di Lammermoor, composed in 1835 to a libretto by Salvatore Cammarano, the house poet of the Naples opera, is based on Sir Walter Scott's novel *The Bride of Lammermoor*. The plot involves two feuding families, the Ashtons and the Ravenswoods: Lucy Ashton has secretly fallen in love with Edgar Ravenswood, but her brother, Henry, has forced her to marry one of his friends, Arthur Bucklaw. The strain proves too much for Lucy, who breaks down under the pressure and goes insane. This gives rise to the famous "Mad Scene" in Act III, a great bravura piece emphasizing coloratura.[1]

The selection here, the sextet, occurs earlier in the action, at a critical point just before the wedding. Henry and Arthur await Lucy, who enters and hesitatingly signs the wedding contract, whereupon the long-missing Edgar suddenly appears and demands satisfaction from Lucy. The various conflicting attitudes are expressed in the sextet proper: Edgar and Henry seek vengeance, Lucy laments her betrayal of Edgar and desires death, and the others hope for mercy and comment on the situation. However, the mood of the music bears little relation to all this. Donizetti simply offers intense melodicism, supported by a sonorous accompaniment of clearly articulated unambiguous harmonies. This lack of affective propriety, as it were, between the dramatic situation and the character of the music is often encountered in opera of the time.

The sextet itself follows a simple structural plan, with two large sections, each consisting of two melodic strains, followed by a coda. Changes in the dramatic action are reflected by alteration in the style and character of the music. They follow quickly upon one another and provide strong contrast. The following outlines the excerpt:

---

[1] Reprinted in MO.

Bar Number	Tempo and Key	Musical Style and Form	Plot
1	Maestoso, C	Recitative	Henry and Arthur await Lucy
8	Moderato, D	*Parlante* (binary arrangement, separated by 4 bars of arioso)	
45		Chorus	
50	Andante, C	*Parlante* and ensemble, later recitative	Lucy enters and signs the contract (note how music breaks off as she does so)
76	Allegro, A♭	Tutti	Entrance of Edgar
99	Larghetto, D♭	Sextet, later with chorus: First section	
133		Second section	
157		Coda	

DONIZETTI: *Lucia di Lammermoor*, Act II, Recitative and Sextet, "Chi mi frena in tal momento"

135

Bellini: "Me chiami, o Norma," Scene and Duet from *Norma*, Act II

Bellini's works differ from those of his contemporaries in several ways. Unlike Rossini, he devoted himself to serious and tragic subjects; unlike Donizetti, he achieved sobriety and dignity. His most successful opera, *Norma*, was composed in 1831 to a text by Felice Romani and is set during the Roman occupation of Gaul in the first century B.C. At its heart is the familiar lover's triangle: Norma, in violation of her vows as high priestess, is in love with the Roman proconsul Pollione, who in turn has fallen in love with Adalgisa, a virgin of the temple. At the tragic climax Norma displays the virtue of *magnanimitas* (magnanimity), so important in the *opera seria* of the previous century. She renounces her love for Pollione, confesses all to her people, and is finally joined in self-sacrifice by the repentant Pollione. In this excerpt Norma, having decided to end her life, tries to persuade Adalgisa to take with her and care for the children she (Norma) has had with Pollione. The remorseful Adalgisa refuses. Structurally, the excerpt follows the most important formal scheme in the Italian opera of the time:

- *Recitative*, stating the dramatic situation
- *Aria*, in slow or moderate tempo, presenting the main character's response (often a *cavatina*, an aria to a short text)
- *Recitative*, bringing a change in the situation
- *Cabaletta*, a fast number, popular in character, often strophic, expressing a new resolve

The scene reprinted here, although described in the score as scene and duet, incorporates all four elements except that duets take the place of arias. The term *scena* ("scene") at the time denoted *recitativo accompagnato*. The excerpt may be outlined as follows:

Bar Number	Section, Marking, and Key	Style Type and Form	Plot
1	I Largo, later Allegro risoluto, *Bb*	Recitative	Norma begs Adalgisa to take the children
	II Allegro moderato, C	Duet, Part I:	
37		Duet	Norma presses her request
103		Arioso	Adalgisa will try to persuade Pollione to return to Norma Adalgisa refuses to leave Norma
121	Andante, *F*	Duet, Part II	Adalgisa claims Pollione loves Norma once more
154	III Allegro, later Lento, *F*	Recitative (also arioso)	Adalgisa succeeds in persuading Norma to go back to Pollione
184	IV Allegro, *F*	Cabaletta	Resolution: agreement

Throughout we can observe the sobriety of Bellini's style, the avoidance of melodrama and intensity, the reticence in orchestration, and the clear, regular harmonic and melodic structure. The first part of the duet proper, Allegro moderato (b. 37 ff.) reveals the traditional aaba scheme with phrases of four bars, followed by a short melodic coda emphasizing sequences and melismatic declamation. Essentially the same scheme is found in the second part of the duet, Andante (b. 121 ff.). The cabaletta is binary, the same text in both parts. A further conservative trait of Bellini is his use of the traditional melodic cadence of the falling fourth in the recitatives. Also characteristic of Bellini are, as Verdi referred to them, the "long, long melodies" and his "individual melancholy."[1] Although most of the ornamentation is to be improvised, the cadenza at the end of the cabaletta is written out.[2]

[1] Verdi, *Letters*, ed. C. Osborne (London: Gollancz, 1971), 263.
[2] The famous aria "Casta diva," from Act I, is reprinted in MO and *NAWM*.

BELLINI: *Norma,* Act II, Scene and Duet, "Me chiami, o Norma"

RECITATIVO.

DUETTO.

Meyerbeer: *Le Prophète*, excerpt from Act IV Finale

The term *grand opera* is used here in its strict sense, to describe a type of French opera that flourished from the late 1820s until the 1860s. It specialized in plots derived from historical events on a grand scale and utilized the most extravagant aspects of the set designer's art. The conclusion of Auber's *La Muette di Portici* of 1828—one of the first grand operas—called for the eruption of Vesuvius, with a great shower of rocks to fall upon the stage. Scenes of great ceremony featured large crowds and long processions, and a ballet was mandatory. Accordingly, large vocal and instrumental forces were necessary. The five-act scheme of French classical tragedy was also employed, as if to lend the weight of historical precedent to the enterprise. Thus grand opera was a worthy counterpart to the large paintings of Géricault and Delacroix and the action-filled dramas of Hugo.

Noted composers of grand operas include Auber, Rossini, Adam, and Halévy, but the primary exponent of the art was Meyerbeer. In collaboration with the librettist Eugène Scribe, he produced a series of works that established him among the leading composers of Europe.

Le Prophète, which was first produced in 1849, recounts the story of Jean (John) of Leyden and the Anabaptist theocracy in Münster in 1534, with a libretto that takes great liberties with history. It centers on the relationship between Jean, his mother, Fidès, and his betrothed, Bertha. Early in the action, Jean, a simple innkeeper, is forced to surrender Bertha to the tyrannical Count Oberthal as ransom for his mother, who has been seized by the Count. Now easy prey for the Anabaptists, Jean is convinced by them to believe that he is the God-King, whose coming has been prophesied. Later Jean's role as prophet forces him to deny that Fidès is his mother and leaves him open to betrayal. The opera concludes in typical grand-opera fashion, with the burning palace collapsing about him.

In this excerpt from the climactic scene near the end of Act IV, Jean enters the cathedral after the march to the portals, is hailed by the multitude, and then is recognized by Fidès. Because acknowledging her to be his mother would place his position in jeopardy, he first denies that he knows her and then declares her to be insane. The excerpt ends in conflict, with Fidès in despair, outrage from Jean and the Anabaptists, and confusion among the onlookers.

These rapidly changing moods—Scribe's stock in trade—are framed and interrupted by passages for the chorus, frequently set with considerable grandeur. Changes in musical style accompany each step of the action. Note the use of the *stile antico*, reminiscent of the religious music of the Renaissance, in the children's chorus and in the full acclamation of Jean the Prophet. This is followed by the disbelieving hesitance in his recitative ("Jean, tu régneras") and Fidès's passionate reply. A short vigorous theme is prominent (first at b. 149), but note that, as with Donizetti's sextet, this theme is independent of the prevailing emotional context. It is in fact used several times during the number, each time with different textual associations: first for indignant reproach, then sympathy, and finally (in a portion not included here) for her eventual agreement with Jean. A final aspect of the music is its emphasis on recitative rather than aria, a characteristic of French opera in general.

The excerpt may be outlined thus:

Bar Number	Section		Tempo and Key	Description
1	I	A	Andantino, D (later A)	Triumphal entrance of Jean, preceded by chorus (with children), soloists, and organ
91		B	——	Recitative of Jean ("Jean, tu régneras"); Fidès recognizes him
122	II	A	Allegro agitato, Ab/ab	Arioso for Fidès ("Je suis, hélas"): distraught, she reveals herself as Jean's mother; note first appearance of main theme at b 149 ("L'ingrat, il ne me reconnaît pas")
159		B	Maestoso, Ab	Chorus with solos; Jean seeks a way out
172		C	Allegretto agitato, ab/Ab	Leads to restatement of Fidès's arioso, this time with chorus, then varied and extended, leading to climax; note use of main theme at b 243 ("Malheur à lui, que sur sa tetê coupable")

In II C, the thematic motives and changing harmonies combine to make a grand effect. Commencing (b. 187 ff.) in E (even though the key signature is Ab), the harmony shifts to D (via Eb = D♯), then G. It then makes a detour via diminished-seventh chords to A, which alternates with the dominant seventh chord in Bb (nonfunctional relationship, b. 226 ff.), culminating in the statement of the theme in the main key, Ab (b. 243 ff.). This is followed by yet another detour through rapidly changing keys, some in nonfunctional relations (Db—F♯—C—Eb and back to Ab, but deceptively, via C).

TRANSLATION

Children's choir (later full chorus):
   Here is the prophet-king,
   here is the Son of God;
   to your knees, bow your head
   before his scepter of fire.
   Bow before his scepter of fire.

Solo:
   O great wonder!
   No woman bore or conceived him.
   Bow to your knees. [Repeated.]

Jean:
   Jean, you are the ruler, ah!
   It is time after all,
   yes, I am the chosen one;
   I am the Son of God.

Fidès:
   My son!

Chorus:
   Her son?

Mathiesèn (to Jean):
   Say the word and she's dead.

Jean:

Who is this woman?

Fidès:

Who am I? me? who am I? me? who
am I?
I am—alas—the poor woman
who nourished you in her arms,
who cried over you called you,
pleaded with you,
who loves no one here below but
you.
Alas! alas! you do not know me, do
not know me, ah!
The wretch! he does not recognize
me,
he does not recognize me, ah, the
wretch! [etc.]

Anabaptists (Chorus):

Heavens, that we must bear this
shameful fraud.
Go away! the prophet will punish
you.

Chorus of people:

What must we hear? Oh heavens!
What a mystery!

Jean (troubled):

What distraction is abusing her
soul?
I do not know any more than you do
what this woman wants.
Must we believe this confession?

Fidès:

What I want?
Alas! what would the poor woman
want?
She would like to pardon the wretch,
she would, even at the price of her
soul,
like a minute to embrace him in her
arms.

(From here on, all sing variously,
together and separately.)

Fidès:

Alas! the wretch does not recognize
me.
Who am I? [etc. Near the end:]
My son lost to me! O frightful fate!
[etc.]

Crowd:

Ah heavens!
The divine prophet suffers too
much
from her blasphemy and delusion.
What a thing!

Main characters, leading citizens
and Anabaptists:

Ah! it is too much for the divine
prophet to suffer
from her blasphemy and delusion.
Turn her over to us, that on her
head,
our anger may at last strike.

Children:

Heavens, what must we hear?
what a confession!

Jonas:

Frightful blasphemy!

Chorus:

What? could the holy prophet
be an imposter?
Woe to him,
that on his guilty head
our anger may at last strike,
our just rage.

Leading citizens:

Heaven's chosen one, the holy
prophet,
could he be an imposter?
Woe to him [etc.]

MEYERBEER: *Le Prophète,* Act IV, excerpt from Finale

(Tout le monde se prosterne. Jean seul, debout sur le haut du grand escalier, descend lentement quelques marches d'un air pensif, puis il porte la main à sa couronne, et dit à voix basse, se rappelant la prédiction du deuxième Acte :)

(Fidès hors d'elle même se frappe les mains;elle veut parler, mais le saisissement lui coupe la parole.)

117
FIDES.
(d'une voix tremblante.) *(avec indignation.)* *(avec une douloureuse tendresse, et en pleurant.)*

Qui je suis? moi! qui je suis? moi! qui je suis?

PIANO.
(M. 69 = ♩)
Allegro agitato.

123

(d'une voix suffoquée par les larmes)
dolce.

Je suis hé -

diminuendo poco a poco.

Ped.

127

_las je suis la pau_vre fem _ me qui t'a nour_ri t'a porté dans ses

206

245

255

262

266

3

The Middle Phase in Germany and Austria

Musical life in nineteenth-century Germany was characterized by a basic division between a progressive group, known as the Neo-Germanic school, which affirmed the new Romantic music, and a traditionalist group, which adhered to the compositional ideals of the late eighteenth and early nineteenth century. This division grew gradually over the first two thirds of the century. The four composers represented in this chapter will be viewed in the context of this division.

Franz Liszt (1811–1886), the internationally celebrated pianist, composer, conductor, and writer, played a central role in establishing the Neo-Germanic tradition. Taking his cue from Berlioz, he composed instrumental works based on subjects from literature and art, devising new musical forms that matched his expressive purposes. In the few cases when he composed in a traditional genre, as in the piano concerto (see the discussion in this chapter) or piano sonata, he altered it radically.

Richard Wagner (1813–1883), who has been regarded as the single most representative Romantic artist, went even further, to develop a new and personal conception of opera in his "art work of the future," as he brought the primary arts together into a single work known as the *Gesamtkunstwerk (universal artwork)*.[1] From the standpoint of repertory this represented something new. In effect Wagner applied the techniques of thematic development and transformation, both associated primarily with instrumental music, to opera, thus creating a new musico-dramatic genre that has come to be known as *music drama*. Moreover, Wagner wrote both libretto and music for these music dramas. He intended this *Gesamtkunstwerk* to supersede all other types of art. For him it represented the end product of all artistic evolution.

Johannes Brahms (1833–1897), by way of contrast, appears as the great traditionalist, who espoused the older ideals of Haydn, Mozart, Beethoven, and Schubert. Brahms rejected the Neo-Germanic repertory of program music and music drama in favor of traditional types such as string quartets, piano sonatas, and symphonies. Thus he has come to be regarded by many as the principal exponent of the classical tradition in nineteenth-century German music.

The work of Anton Bruckner (1824–1896), the deeply religious rural Austrian, presents problems of interpretation in the context of the basic division. He is generally

---

[1] See J. Barzun, *Darwin, Marx, Wagner: Critique of a Heritage*, 2nd ed. (Garden City: Anchor, 1958), to which the following is indebted.

considered part of the Neo-Germanic group, since his expressive intentions were frequently realized through the use of musical styles that had explicit extramusical, often programmatic, associations and through his employment, particularly in the later works, of a greatly enlarged orchestra. Yet in the center of his work—the symphony—he remained close to traditional concepts; that is, he did not compose "program symphonies," and like Brahms, he was scarcely involved with literary matters.

Section One: Liszt

"Vallée d'Obermann", from *Années de pèlerinage*, 1, *Suisse* (S. 160, no. 6)[1]

This large-scale character piece is related both to Liszt's sojourn in Switzerland in 1835–1836 with the Countess Marie d'Agoult and to the novel *Obermann*, by Étienne de Sénancour, originally published in 1804. Liszt presumably composed the piece while in Switzerland, but did not publish it until 1840, in a set called *Impressions et Poésies*, the first volume of a projected series with the general title *Album d'un voyageur* (S. 156). The title was later changed to *Années de pèlerinage*.[2]

Sénancour's *Obermann* concerns a sensitive man who leaves urban life to wander in a remote area, eventually settling in an isolated Swiss mountain valley. In a letter to his publisher Liszt emphasized Obermann's doubts and despair concerning life and civilization, characterizing the novel as "the monochord of the unrequited loneliness of human suffering . . . in a bleak, desiccated and sublime book." He went on to describe his composition as a "sombre, hyper-elegiac fragment . . . a desolate sorrow-landscape."[3]

Vallée d'Obermann is prefaced by quotations from the novel as well as from Byron's *Childe Harold's Pilgrimage*.

From Sénancour:

> What do I want? What am I? What may I demand of nature? . . . All cause is invisible, all effect misleading; every form changes, all time runs its course . . . I feel, I exist only to exhaust myself in untameable desires, to drink deep of the allurement of a fantastic world, only to be finally vanquished by its sensuous illusion (from Letter 63).

> All the ineffable sensibility, the charm, and the torment of our barren years; the vast consciousness of Nature, everywhere overwhelming, and everywhere unfathomable, universal love, indifference, ripe wisdom, sensuous ease—all that a mortal heart can contain of desire and profound sorrow, I felt them all, experienced them all on that memorable night; I have made an ominous stride towards the age of failing powers; I have consumed ten years of my life (from Letter 4).

---

[1] The "S" numbers refer to the listing of Liszt's works compiled by H. Searle, *Grove's Dictionary of Music and Musicians*, 5th ed., iv (1954) and used again in *The New Grove Dictionary of Music and Musicians*, ix (1980).

[2] In the early 1850s, when he had given up the career of traveling virtuoso and had settled in Weimar, Liszt set about systematically preparing many of his compositions for publication. At this time he settled on the title for this set. It originally consisted of two volumes, *Suisse* (S. 160) and *Italie* (S. 161), published in 1855 and 1858 respectively; a third volume, *Italie*, was added later. In the anthologies: *Sonetto 104 del Petrarca* from *Italie* is in MSO and NSe; *Sonetto 123 del Petrarca* from the same set is in CSM. Examples of Liszt's prose may be found in *MWW*.

[3] See F. E. Kirby, "Liszt's Pilgrimage," *PQ* 89 (23rd Year, Spring 1975): 20.

From Byron (III, xcvii):

> Could I embody and unbosom now
>   That which is most within me,—could I wreak
> My thoughts upon expression, and thus throw
> Soul—heart—mind—passions—feelings, strong or weak—
> All that I would have sought, and all I seek—
> Bear, know, feel—and yet breathe,—into *one* word,
> And that one word were Lightning, I would speak;
> But as it is, I live and die unheard,
> With a voiceless thought, sheathing it as a sword.

Vallée d'Obermann displays a free sectional form that corresponds to no traditional structural plan. Its form, rather, derives from Liszt's interpretation of Sénancour's novel and is unique to this composition. There are four sections (see the outline that follows the discussion), which seem to portray in turn Obermann's melancholy brooding (I), his serenity in the mountain valley (II), the intensity of his despair (III), and, finally, his triumph (IV). One must say "seem to," for there are no specific correlations between the quotations used as captions (quoted previously) and the piece itself. For instance, the quotations do not in any way convey the triumphant affirmation implied at the end of the piece. The piece also disregards traditional tonal structure by not beginning and ending in the same key.

Alternation between points of intensity and repose is important in the piece. Toward the end of II, a climax is evidently building (b. 103 ff.), but dissipates, and a solo line (unmeasured) leads to the sudden onset of recitative. Section IV corresponds thematically to II, but here the climax is achieved.

Another notable characteristic of *Vallée d'Obermann*—and of much Romantic music—is its use of thematic transformation. At first it seems that three separate themes are employed in the piece: the first melancholy (a quality enhanced by the unresolved sevenths), the second serene at first (note the effective use of the treble register) but later triumphant, and the third an impassioned recitative. Yet all three prove to be interrelated, sharing common elements that allow the piece to be regarded as monothematic.

The exploitation of styles borrowed from opera is an aspect of nineteenth-century instrumental music not often fully appreciated. The most striking manifestation here is the turbulent recitative (III), which employs Liszt's virtuosic style in the form of fast passages in octaves accompanied by tremolo chords. The crescendo and acceleration in this passage coupled with numerous and at times extravagant expressive markings link it with the *recitativo accompagnato* of serious opera, traditionally reserved for the expression of the most extreme feelings. The aesthetics of this work are also derived from opera: Seriousness and intensity are associated with virtuosity. Finally, the reliance on lyrical melody with accompaniment—admittedly prevalent during the period—surely has antecedents in opera, too.

Vallée d'Obermann can be outlined as follows (the second statement of I is not an exact repetition):

Bar Number	Section, Marking, and Key			Themes	Character
1	I	a:	Lento assai, g/G	1A	Lyric, melancholy
8		b:	sotto voce	2A	
25		c:	Più lento	3A	
34		a:	Tempo I	1A	
41		b:	espressivo	2A	
59		c:	Più lento	3A	
74	II		Un poco più di moto ma sempre lento, C	B	Lyric, serene
119	III		Recitativo, e	C	Passionate intensity
170	IV		Lento, E	B	Lyric: first serene, then triumphant

LISZT: Annèes de pélerinage, 1, Suisse, "Vallée d'Obermann" (S. 160, no. 6)

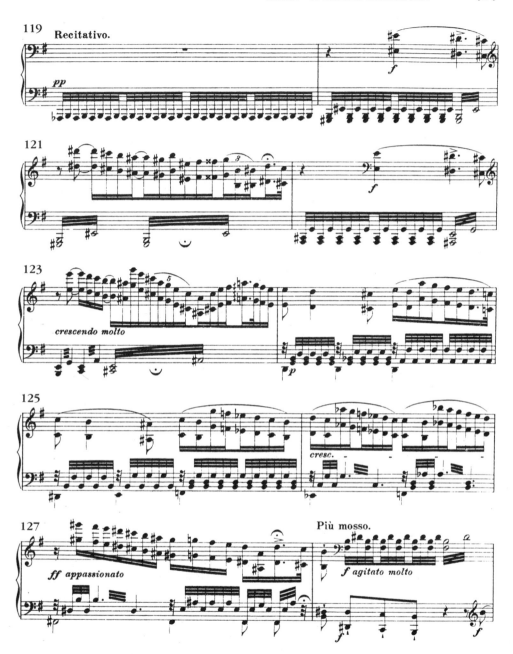

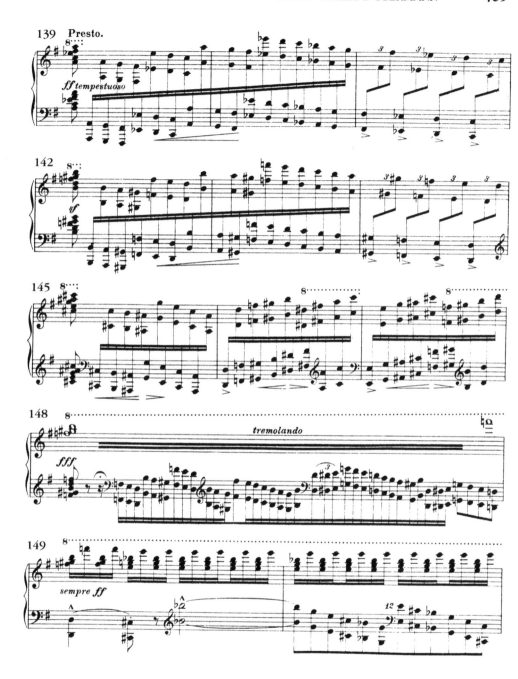

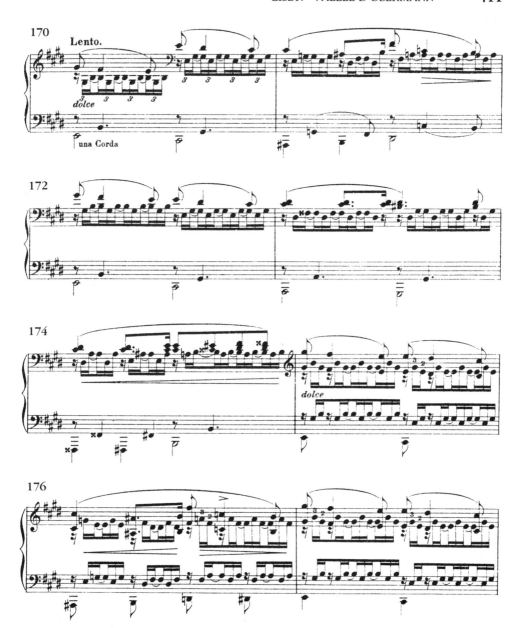

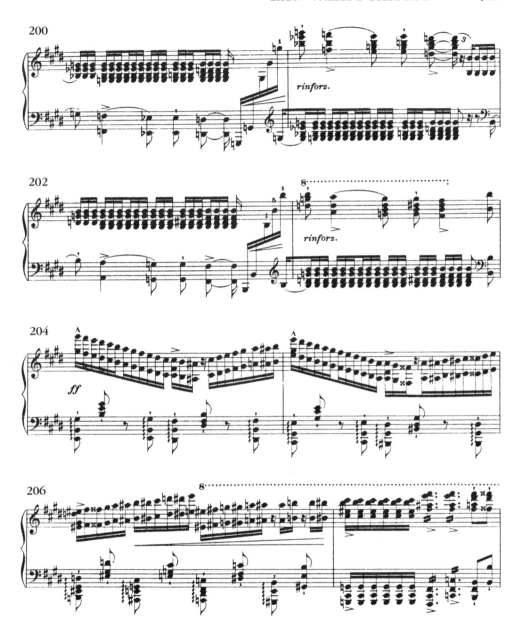

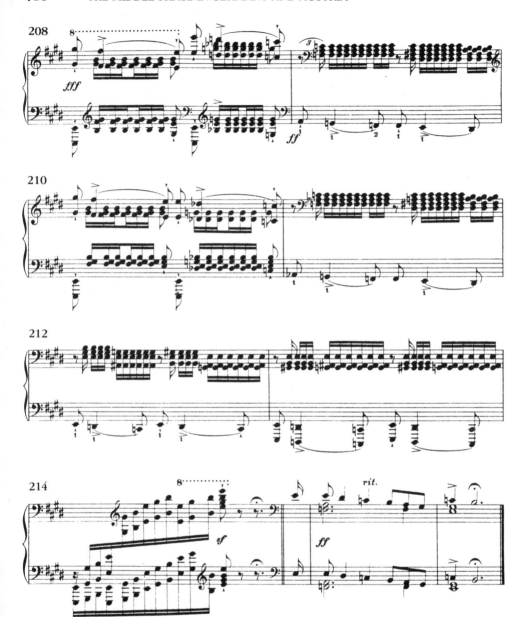

Piano Concerto No. 1 in E♭ (S. 124)

Both of Liszt's piano concertos, like *Vallée d'Obermann*, were revised and published during his time in Weimar. The first, reprinted here, was presumably sketched in part around 1830, completed in 1849, revised in 1853 and again in 1856, and published in 1857. Such a complicated history is characteristic of Liszt's compositions.

The concerto is particularly notable for its cyclic form with thematic transformation on an unprecedently comprehensive scale, its variety in expressive character, and its rhetorical grandiloquence, which frequently calls for great virtuosity and power from the soloist. It displays an elaborate orchestration, including trombones, piccolo, cymbals, and triangle—the use of the latter provides the nickname for the piece. Despite this full instrumentation the work still preserves Mozart's concept of *primus inter pares* (first among equals) in the relationship between solo and tutti, although with much greater contrast between the two. Indeed, the work could well have been called *concerto symphonique*, following the example of Henri Litolff, a music publisher and composer who used the title for concertos in the 1840s and 1850s.

Unlike most concertos, Liszt's piece is in four interconnected movements that correspond to those found in many sonatas and symphonies: I, Allegro maestoso, E♭; II, Quasi Adagio, B; III, Allegretto vivace, E♭ (e♭ is prominent); and IV, Allegro marziale animato, E♭. The overall form of the work is ambiguous. It can be viewed as either consisting of four movements or as being in a single movement with four sections. In any case, the movements (sections) are short and their forms much freer than was customary. Coherence is achieved through the cyclic form.

Most significant in the work as a whole is the motivic opening theme, with its dotted rhythms and chromatic descent. Liszt once humorously characterized this theme with the expression "das versteht Ihr alle nicht" ("none of you will understand this"),[1] to which it can be sung. The theme is presented transformed at the end of the movement (b. 118) in an impressive passage in which the soloist is accompanied by sustained winds and timpani, a section doubtless modeled on the conclusion of the finale of Beethoven's *Emperor* Concerto, which is in the same key. The theme also appears in a recapitulating passage, but mostly in the "wrong" key, near the end of the third movement (b. 134), in preparation for the onset of the finale. It last appears at the very end of the work (finale, b. 131), when it emerges as the climax of a long crescendo.

The fourth movement is derived mostly from themes of the second, from which its principal theme and that of the important recitative passage were taken. But the main theme of the third movement also puts in an appearance (b. 88). In its use of cyclic form and thematic transformation the work resembles Liszt's character pieces and symphonic poems; the only thing lacking is the program itself. A model for the concerto may have been provided by Schubert's *Wanderer* Fantasia for piano (D. 760), a virtuoso piece with cyclic form, which Liszt knew well (he prepared a version of it for piano and orchestra). Another well-known example of such comprehensive cyclic organization is Schumann's Symphony 4, d (op. 120).[2] Despite these

---

[1] Quoted by R. Collet, *Franz Liszt: The Man and his Music*, ed. A. Walker (New York: Taplinger, 1970), 260.

[2] Reprinted in S.

precedents, Liszt drew attention to the novelty of his procedure: "This way of bringing together and rounding off at the close," he wrote in a letter, "is pretty much my own; from the standpoint of musical form it can readily be maintained and justified."[3]

The forms used in the individual movements are decidedly untraditional. The structural types standard in concertos—the sonata-related form of the first movement, the aria-like arrangements found in the slow movement, and the rondo characteristic of the finale—are replaced by sectional forms.

The concerto exhibits a great range of expressive character, from its terse, motivic principal theme, to the nocturne-like themes of the first and second movements, where the accompaniment to the piano often features a solo instrument. Passages of great virtuosity include the cadenzas in the first and third movements, which Liszt, departing from earlier practice, wrote out in full. The writing for the piano abounds in octave passages, arpeggio figurations, trills, scales, rapid chords, and the like. Frequently free rhythm ("senza misura") is suggested by the absence of bar lines, particularly in the recitatives.

[3]Letter of 26 March 1857; see *Briefwechsel zwischen Franz Liszt und Hans von Bülow*, ed. La Mara (Leipzig: Breitkopf & Härtel, 1898), 248.

LISZT: Piano Concerto No. 1 in E♭ (S. 124)

419

69

79

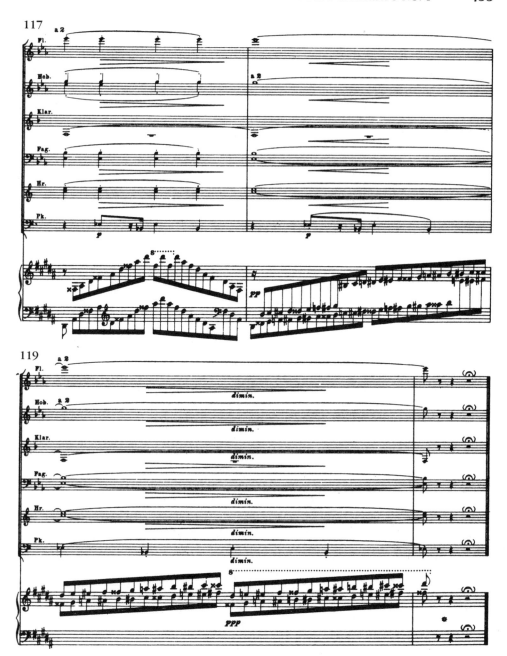

163

170

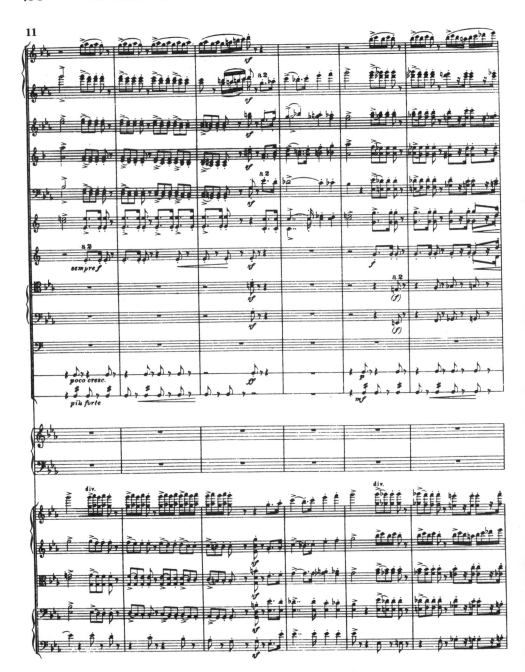

133

142

147

153

Section Two: Wagner

Excerpt beginning "O merke wohl, was ich dir melde!" from *Die Walküre*, Act I

Immediately after completing his major theoretical writings in the early 1850s Wagner began his most ambitious project, *Der Ring des Nibelungen (The Ring of the Nibelung)*. This expansive work, consisting of four music dramas, is organized as a trilogy with prologue, based on medieval epics from Germany and Iceland, the *Nibelungenlied*[1] and *Edda* legends. The *Ring* was not completed until 1874.[1] It presents a monumental tale of rise, decline, fall, and redemption, ranging in locale between the German mythological equivalents of Heaven (*Walhall*, Valhalla) and Hell (*Nibelheim*).

While it is impossible to include the full plot here, the dramatic situation of the excerpt can be summarized.[2] Wotan, chief among the gods, attempts better to secure his interests by going among men disguised as Wälse. There he has sired twins, Siegmund and Sieglinde, who are known as the Wälsungs, and who are left to grow up in the woods apart from society. As *Die Walküre* begins, Siegmund, fleeing his enemies, has arrived at Hunding's house, where he meets Sieglinde, now Hunding's wife. The twins gradually become more attracted to each other. Hunding, who also proves to be among Siegmund's enemies, orders his weaponless guest to defend himself the following morning. When Hunding has retired, Sieglinde tells Siegmund the story of the sword in the tree (see translation). Siegmund then successfully extracts the sword, and, after a moment of recognition, the twins decide to escape together.

This excerpt contains Sieglinde's narrative, Siegmund's rejoinder and his lyrical "Spring Song."

It also provides a good example of Wagner's early approach to the multiple elements that form a *Gesamtkunstwerk*, at a time when he still felt that the different art forms, notably music and poetry, should be on an equal footing. Specifically this means the recitative and the aria, poetry dominant in the former, music in the latter. Wagner brought the two together by means of a new melodic styles, *Sprechgesang* (tone-speech), which incorporates elements of both. This style is well represented in Sieglinde's narrative, and Siegmund's "Spring Song" shows it at its most melodious, a virtual aria. The *Sprechgesang* can encompass considerable variety. In this style the whole is continuously composed: The traditional divisions between separate numbers have been eliminated.

---

[1] The individual music dramas (dates refer to composition) are: *Rheingold* (1853–1854), *Die Walküre* (1854–1856), *Siegfried* (1856–1869, with small additions in 1871), and *Götterdämmerung* (1869–1874). An excerpt from Act II of *Siegfried* is in MO, and the final scene of *Götterdämmerung* (Brünnhilde's Immolation) is in CSM (piano reduction in both cases).

[2] See F. E. Kirby, *An Introduction to Western Music: Bach, Beethoven, Wagner, Stravinsky* (New York: Free Press, 1970), 318–27, as well as E. Newman, *The Wagner Operas* (New York: Knopf, 1972; originally published in 1949). On Wagner's theories and aesthetics, see J. Stein, *Richard Wagner and the Synthesis of the Arts* (Detroit: Wayne State University Press, 1960). Excerpts from Wagner's writings are in MWW and SRMH.

A second element is the use of *leitmotivs,* short musical motives associated with characters or other aspects of the work, which provide the basic thematic material (see Example 1). Note the appositeness with which they are employed, especially the inclusion in Sieglinde's narrative of the Valhalla theme, in reference to Wotan, disguised as Wälse, and the Sword theme.

Finally one must refer to the scoring, a central element in Romantic music generally. Only a few aspects of this will be pointed out in this excerpt: the use of the ceremonial wind-band, reminiscent of what accompanied Sarastro in Mozart's *Die Zauberflöte,*[3] for the first statement of the Valhalla theme (later strings are used); solo horns and later trumpet for the forceful and fanfare-like Sword theme; harps and a long line for the cellos to introduce Siegmund's "Spring Song"; the combination of flute, oboe, and clarinets for the Love theme; and so on.

EXAMPLE 1.   LEITMOTIVS, *DIE WALKURE,* ACT I

For the most part, Wagner's treatment of harmony is conventional here. His extensive use of seventh and ninth chords can scarcely be considered radical. Large sections of the excerpt remain in a single key, e–E for Sieglinde's narrative, g–G for the rejoicing of the twins, and B♭ for Siegmund's "Spring Song." But note at the opening of the door, which takes place at the climax of a crescendo, how the change in mood is underlined by a change in harmony (via the diminished-seventh chord and enharmonic relations). The key signature of G/e is maintained in the vocal part while in the orchestra that of B♭ is introduced. This transformation is reminiscent of the beginning of the aria in Weber's *Freischütz* (see the first selection, "Wie nahte mir der Schlummer," in Chapter 1, b. 13–15). Near the conclusion of the "Spring Song," however, the harmony becomes much less stable, reflecting not only the uncertain and doubtful state in which the twins find themselves but also the love they increasingly feel for each other. Throughout the excerpt Wagner frequently uses nonfunctional stepwise progressions, as from B^7 or D^7 to C.

Although's Wagner's music appears—and often is—through-composed, standard forms of various types can often be recognized in it. The most detailed analysis of Wagner based on this premise was carried out in the 1920s by Alfred Lorenz.[4] Lorenz asserted that a variety of formal schemes, based mostly either on the *Bogen* (bow or arch, aba) or the *Bar* (aab), or some variant of either, constituted the formal building blocks of Wagner's music. This interpretation is no longer accepted, although the first part of the excerpt, Sieglinde's narrative, clearly falls into the familiar three-part form (*Bogen*), with the first part in two subsections. The next passage, however, falls into two parts, the first for Sieglinde and the second for Siegfried, which are not sufficiently parallel to be considered strophes, as Lorenz would suggest. Similarly, Siegmund's "Spring Song" is in two sections but cannot really be regarded as strophic. The following outlines the excerpt:

Bar Number	Section	Tempo and Key	Style	Leitmotiv
	I: Sieglinde's Narrative			
1	Introduction		Recitative	
5	A 1	Langsamer, e	Recitative	
13	2	Mässig, E	Arioso	Valhalla
27	B	——, E–e	Arioso	Sword
53	A 1	——, e	Recitative	Sword
62	2	Ruhig, E	Arioso	Valhalla
72	II: Rejoicing of the Wälsungs	Sehr lebhaft, G	Arioso	Sword Wälsung's Cry of Victory
137	III: Opening of the door	Tempo I, F♯/G♭	Mixed	
	IV: Siegmund's Spring Song			
149	Introduction	Mässig bewegt, Bb	Orchestra	
157	A	Sehr fliessendes Tempo, Bb	Aria (free form)	Spring song
186	B	——		Love

[4] A. Lorenz, *Das Geheimnis der Form bei Richard Wagner*, 4 vols. (Berlin: Hesse, 1924–33/R 1966); see the summary of *Die Walküre* in G. Abraham, *A Hundred Years of Music* (London: Duckworth, 1938/R Chicago: Aldine, 1964), 122.

TRANSLATION

Sieglinde:
    Pay attention to what I say.
    All the relatives
    were sitting here in the hall,
    invited by Hunding to the wedding.
    He was marrying a woman [—me—]
    who against her will
    had been given to him
    as wife by thieves.
    Sad, I sat there
    while they were drinking:
    A stranger entered,
    an old man, dressed in gray,
    his hat pulled down over his head;
    it covered one of his eyes,
    but the light of the other
    struck terror in everyone
    as its powerful threat
    struck at the men;
    only in me
    did that glance awake
    a sweet and yearning sorrow,
    tears and comfort at the same time.
    He looked at me
    and glared at them
    as he swung a sword in his hands
    and that he struck
    into the ash tree's trunk,
    driving it up to the handle.
    This steel should belong to
    whoever could pull it from the tree.
    All the men
    —as bravely as they tried—
    the weapon was won by none.
    Guests came
    and guests went,
    the strongest pulled at the steel—
    no tribute could be
    drawn from the tree:
    There silent the sword remained.
    Then I knew who it was
    who greeted my miserable self:
    I also know
    for whom, alone,
    he intended the sword in the tree.

Oh, if I could find him, my friend,
and if he were here today!
If he came from far away
to the most miserable woman:
whatever I have suffered
in the most bitter sorrow,
whatever has pained me
in shame and humiliation—
the sweetest revenge
would make up for everything.
I would then have recovered
what I had lost,
what I had wept over
would be mine once more,
if I could find this holiest of friends
and embrace the hero!

Siegmund:
    Dearest woman,
    you now have found your friend,
    destined for woman and weapon.
    Hot in my bosom
    burns the oath
    which will marry me to
    your noble self.
    Everything I have yearned for
    I now find in you;
    in you I have found
    what was lacking in me!
    If you suffered disgrace,
    I was struck with pain;
    while I was outlawed,
    you were dishonored.
    For joyful revenge
    the happy ones now cry out.
    I will laugh out
    in the holiest of joys
    can I but embrace your sacred self,
    can I but feel your beating heart.

(The door opens.)

Sieglinde:
    Ha, who goes there? who came in?

Siegmund:
    No one went,

but someone came in:
see, Spring
is laughing in the hall.
Winter storms give way to
the wonderful moon,
Spring is glowing in the mild light;
On soft winds, light and lovely
he rocks, wonderfully moving;
through field and forest his
breath is blowing,
his laughing eye is wide open.
From the songs of blessed birds
he sweetly intones,
the most gentle odors
are what he breathes out;
From his warm blood spring forth
wonderful blossoms;
buds and sprouts
spring forth through his might.
With the grace of gentle weapons

he subdues the whole world.
Winter and storm give way
to the powerful weapon;
Thus the brave blows have
forced even the stern doors,
which, spiteful and rigid,
kept us apart from him.
He swept in here
to his sister
Love has attracted Spring here:
in our bosom
it was hidden deep;
Now it can laugh blessedly in the light;
the sister-bride
can woo the brother!
In ruins lies
all that separated them:
joyfully the young couple
greet each other.
Love and Spring are united.

WAGNER: *Die Walküre,* Act I, "O merke wohl, was ich dir melde!"

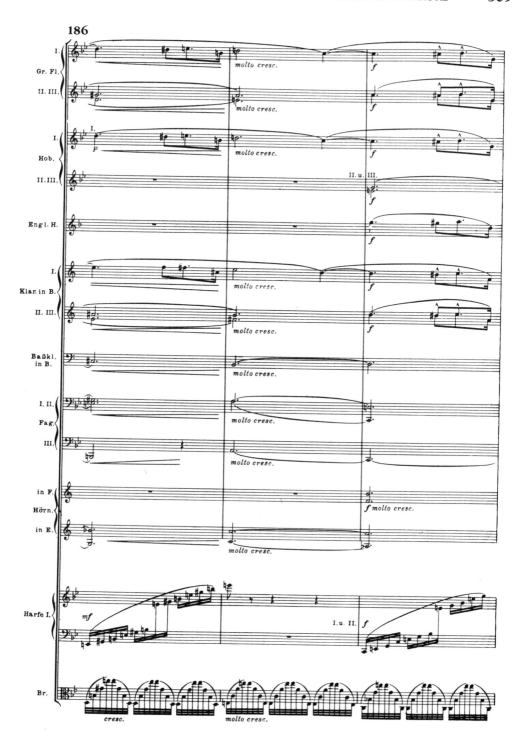

189

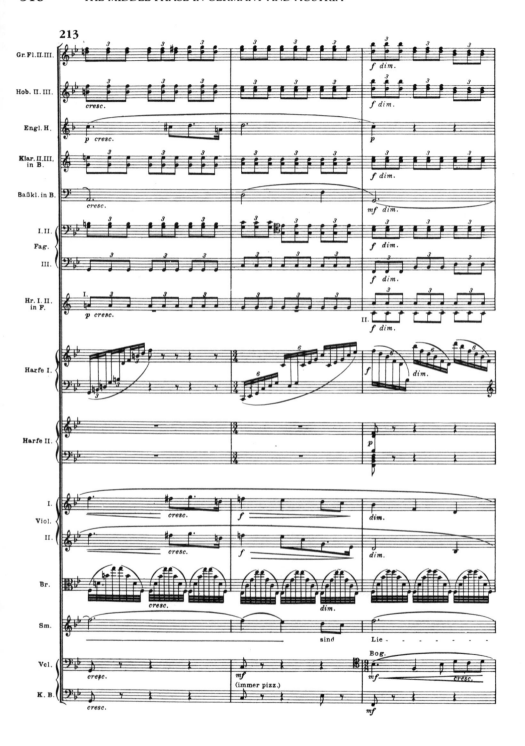

Tristan's Delirium, Excerpt from *Tristan und Isolde,* Act III

Tristan und Isolde was composed in 1857–1859 and first performed in 1865. The story comes from the medieval epic by Gottfried of Strassburg, but, as was his habit, Wagner drastically cut the epic to concentrate on the doomed love between Tristan, a knight of King Arthur's Round Table, and Isolde, an Irish princess married to King Mark of Cornwall, Tristan's liege. The action can be quickly summarized: Tristan escorts his former lover, Isolde, to Cornwall for her wedding to Mark. A love potion given them by Brangäne, Isolde's servant, rekindles this love. Eventually they are discovered by Mark, and Tristan is mortally wounded in the duel that follows. Back at his home and in delirium he awaits the arrival of Isolde, only to die in her arms. She then wills herself to join him in death. The plot allows for a radical emphasis on the inner, or psychological, action (since there is little external action), which Wagner believed to be the most effective area for musical expression.

The text of *Tristan und Isolde* utilizes symbols prominent in German Romantic literature. A primary example is the opposition between *day* and *night: day* represents the world of everyday life, *night* the dark realm of passionate and ecstatic love that finds fulfillment only in death. Renunciation of life, therefore, plays an important role in this work, as elsewhere in Wagner. The day–night symbolism was foreshadowed, for instance, in Novalis's *Hymns of the Night* (1800).

This concentration on the central situation in the plot is matched by concentration in the music. The use of a small number of *leitmotivs* results in the intense, overpowering expression of a single feeling: passionate, all-consuming, ecstatic love. Musically this is accomplished by an emphasis on the incessant repetition of a few short melodic themes and motives, usually in melodic sequences that modulate by ascending half-steps and that are underscored with complex chromatic harmonies featuring unresolved seventh and ninth chords. This imparts a quality of restless striving that never arrives at a point of resolution or stability. Wagner's consistent use of chromatic harmonies and the constant modulation in the context of the intensely passionate character of the expression has come to be known as the "Tristan style." It is particularly evident in Act III.

Our excerpt from the "Delirium Scene" therefore provides a good example of Wagner's late style. Here, under the influence of Schopenhauer, he decided to allow music the dominant role in the constitution of the music drama, in contradistinction to the theories he had formulated in the 1850s. *Tristan und Isolde* is the first complete work in which this approach is evident.[1]

Specific key signatures are indicated—*e* for most of the excerpt, *f* at the end—but Wagner constantly makes references and excursions to other keys, and, moreover, makes frequent use of seventh and ninth chords. Secondary dominants are common. The avoidance of cadences further prevents a feeling of resolution. In Tristan's response to Kurwenal's announcement of Isolde's imminent arrival (b. 45 ff.), the

---

[1] Excerpts in other anthologies include the Prelude to Act I, in AMA, CSM, NSe, MSO and NCS, the last two with the Love-Death (the very end of the work); AMA and NSe contain excerpts from the Love Scene in Act II; NAWM has the potion-drinking scene in Act I; short excerpts are in MO. Wagner's own description of the Prelude to Act I may be found in MWW.

forceful repetitions of the transformed Isolde theme are set to unresolved seventh and ninth chords that strive for a cadence on C, but at the moment of expected resolution the minor-ninth chord on F♯ appears (b. 60), thus setting up a new harmonic situation. Another example is the passage where Tristan believes he sees the arrival of Isolde's ship (b. 123). This begins with the tonic incomplete minor ninth chord in C, followed by a dominant seventh in C, which moves to the C triad but with an added sixth. The subsequent sharping of C leads to a dominant ninth chord in D, and so on, all in an atmosphere of feverish excitement. Complexity and intensity, then, are the hallmarks of this harmonic style.

The part writing is also complex: The voice is often treated simply as an additional part of the entire score, rather than as a main element to be accompanied by the orchestra.[2] Moreover, instead of treating the different sections (strings, winds, brass) as separate entities, as had been customary and is found even in the excerpt from *Die Walküre* (see the preceding excerpt), instruments are freely combined to create unique and evocative sonorities. This is one of the most important features of Wagner's orchestration, and was derived from French and French-influenced music such as that of Berlioz and Liszt. This treatment is evident in the excerpt in the passage where Tristan fervently thanks Kurwenal for his loyal service, (b. 72), with strings and winds presenting the main thematic material.

This complexity and intensity is particularly evident in the treatment of the *leitmotivs*, which Wagner once characterized as

> restlessly emerging, developing, separating, then again reuniting, growing, diminishing, finally clashing, embracing and well-nigh engulfing one another.[3]

The excerpt may be outlined as follows (see Example 2):

Bar	Marking	Plot	Leitmotivs
1	Schnell belebend	Kurwenal's announcement	Isolde (diminution)
			Frau Minne as love
		Tristan's monologue	
45	Sehr lebhaft	I: Longing	Isolde (strong scoring)
72	Etwas mässiger	II: Praise of	Isolde
		Kurwenal	Anguish
115	Lebhaft	III: Longing	Reminiscence from Act II
			Anguish
140		IV: Delusion	Anguish
155	Mässig langsam	Reality	Melancholy piping of
			the shepherd

---

[2] We know that Wagner first sketched his works out as short scores on two or three staff lines, and then elaborated the orchestral parts at a later stage in the process of composition. The recent work on Wagner's sketches has been summarized by R. Bailey, "[Wagner:] The Method of Composition," *The Wagner Companion* (London: Faber & Faber, 1979), 269 ff.

[3] *Schriften*, vii (Leipzig: Siegel, 1907), 186, trans. F. E. K.

EXAMPLE 2.   LEITMOTIVS, *TRISTAN UND ISOLDE*, ACT III (TRISTAN'S DELIRIU

Isolde
(with Tristan)

Sea Voyage
(also known as
Sick Tristan)

Tristan's
Anguish

Reminiscence
from Act II

Frau Minne
as Love

TRANSLATION

Kurwenal:

Since she is still alive
let your hope laugh.
Even though you think
Kurwenal stupid
today you must not scold him.
You've been lying as if dead
since the day
that Melot, crazy,
struck you that wound.
The cruel wound,
how can it be healed?
To me—poor me—
it seemed that she
who healed the wound
caused by Morold
could easily heal the pain
from Melot's weapon.
Thus I found
the best doctor.
I have sent to Cornwall:
a faithful man
will bring Isolde
across the sea to you.

Tristan:

Isolde is coming!
Isolde is approaching!
O true friendship! noble
sweet friendship!
O Kurwenal,
you loyal friend:
faithful, with no hesitation,
how can I thank you?
My shield, my guardian
in battle and strife,
in joy and sorrow, always ready.
Whomever I hated,
you also hated;
whoever was my friend

was your friend too.
To good King Mark,
when I served him well,
you were good as gold.
But when I had to betray
my noble lord,
you willingly did the same!
You serve not yourself,
but me alone;
you suffer along with me
when I suffer;
but what I suffer now,
that you cannot feel.
This fearful longing
which consumes me:
this yearning and burning
that sears me;
could I but tell you,
could you but feel it,
you would not stay here,
you would run to the watch-tower,
seeking with all your might,
with yearning, from here
out there observing, espying,
where the sails are billowing,
where before the wind,
looking for me,
fired by the power of love,
Isolde is sailing to me!
She's coming! she's coming
with joy and speed!
There's waving, waving,
the flag on the mast!
The boat! the boat!
There it goes past the bar!
Don't you see it?
Kurwenal, don't you see it?

Kurwenal:

No ship is there yet.

WAGNER: *Tristan und Isolde,* Act III, Tristan's Delirium

Section Three: Brahms

Songs
A. "Sonntag" (op. 47, no. 3)
B. "Frühlingslied" (op. 85, no. 5)

In the tradition of Schubert and Schumann, Brahms emphasized the vocal line and stressed melodic lyricism in his *Lieder*. But at the same time he reduced the importance of the piano accompaniment, particularly the use of preludes, interludes, and postludes. He also frequently employed strophic form, writing few through-composed songs. Unlike many of his predecessors and contemporaries, Brahms chose his texts mostly from the work of lesser-known poets.

"Sonntag" ("Sunday"), composed in 1860 and published in 1868, has a text taken from a collection of folk-song poems edited by the poet Ludwig Uhland. Accordingly the song shows elements derived from folk songs, such as strict strophic form, regularity of phrase structure (four-bar units) and almost exclusive use of diatonic harmonies. Brahms studied folk songs extensively, making many arrangements of them and incorporating melodies based on them into his instrumental works.[1]

"Frühlingslied" ("Spring Song") was composed in 1878 and published in 1882. It is set to a poem by Emanuel Geibel, a prominent member of the "Munich Circle," whose work aspired to a refined idealized beauty by cultivating older poetic forms while avoiding touches of realism. This aesthetic was not unrelated to that of Brahms himself. In his setting of the poem's three strophes Brahms employs an important variant of the modified strophic form: The middle strophe is set to contrasting music, thus producing the "aba" arrangement, and a coda is also added. Even though it remains of secondary significance, the accompaniment is rich and sonorous and displays Brahms's penchant for rhythmic complexity, emphasizing hemiola and syncopation. This combination of lyricism with rhythmic intricacy is characteristic of Brahms.

---

[1] Another folk-like song, "Vergebliches Ständchen" (op. 84 iv) is in MSO. Other songs in the anthologies include "Die Mainacht" (op. 43 ii) in CSM and "Immer leiser wird mein Schlummer" (op. 105 ii) in MSO.

TRANSLATIONS

A. SUNDAY

Strophe 1

 So I've not seen my darling for a whole week;
 I saw her on a Sunday surely standing by the door,
 the very beautiful girl,
 wish to God I were with her today.

Strophe 2

 So I've not been able to laugh for a whole week;
 I saw her on a Sunday surely standing by the church,
 the very beautiful girl,
 wish to God I were with her today.

B. SPRING SONG

Strophe 1

 With its mysterious odors
 the forest greets me even from the slope;
 above me, on high
 the first larks are soaring.

Strophe 2

 Absorbed in the sweet sound
 I wander slowly through the fields,
 which, still drunk with sleep,
 softly send shoots up toward the light.

Strophe 3

 What a longing! what a dreaming!
 Ah! from your burning-out,
 the trees, the flowers could make you,
 old heart, bloom once more.

BRAHMS: "Sonntag" (op. 47, no. 3)

BRAHMS: "Frühlingslied" (op. 85, no. 5)

Variations on a Theme of Haydn for Orchestra (op. 56a)

Composed in 1873, this work marks Brahms's return to the orchestral medium, for which he had not written since the late 1850s. Having established his reputation through solo piano and chamber music and, particularly, the *German Requiem* (op. 45), he once more sought to engage the most prestigious part of the repertory, pure instrumental music for orchestra. Yet instead of the symphony, Brahms, with typical deference toward tradition, chose something smaller and less prominent in the orchestral repertory: a theme and variations. This work shows Brahms's respect for the past, since it is based on a movement in an eighteenth-century divertimento for woodwind ensemble, the *Chorale St. Antoni,* then thought to have been composed by Haydn, but now considered anonymous.[1] It exists in two versions, one for two pianos, the other for orchestra. Presumably the two-piano version is the earlier—at least it was published first. Moreover, the extant sketches relate mostly to this version.

Not only is the true composer of the *Chorale St. Antoni* unknown, but so is the significance of the title. Most scholars assume it refers to a pilgrimage or penitential ceremony related either to St. Anthony the Great (250–c.350) or St. Anthony of Padua (1195–1231). In any case, the processional character of the theme is clear from the style as well as the form, rounded binary, a structure consistently used for marches in the eighteenth century. The theme may be outlined as follows:

$$\|: a \ a :\| \ \|: b \ c \ a \ d \ e :\|$$

Varying phrase lengths make the theme unusual: "a" is five bars long, "b," "c," and "d" comprise four each, while "e" has but three. Each variation maintains the structure of the theme, as was customary for this form, even though some changes are introduced into what traditionally were exact repetitions. In Variation IV an extra bar is added at the end of the second section.

The statement of the theme is followed by eight variations, each with one or more elements related to the theme, yet each one has its own individual character. Variations IV and VIII are *minore* variations. The march character of the theme reappears in Variations I and VI, and Variation V is a scherzo, while Variation VII employs the rhythm of the sarabande. In Variation III a long melodic line replaces the phrase structure of the original theme.

A finale follows the last variation. It is based on an ostinato, another example of Brahms's interest in earlier techniques. Here the ostinato is a five-bar unit derived from the "a" phrase of the theme. It appears 16 times, usually in the bass, but elsewhere in statements 13–15 (b. 426–40), whereupon (b. 446) the ostinato pattern in abandoned.

For the most part Brahms employs here the standard orchestra disposition of the late eighteenth century: woodwinds and brass in pairs, timpani and strings *a 5* (in five parts). This scoring is similar to that of some of Haydn's London symphonies, as is attested to, for instance, by the absence of trombones. Apart from the piccolo, tri-

---

[1] See generally the excellent edition with commentary by D. McCorkle (*NCS*, 1976), with an extensive bibliography; note particularly the long analysis by L. Stein. Another of Brahms's works based on eighteenth-century music, the Variations and Fugue on a Theme of Handel (op. 24), is excerpted in MSO.

angle, and four horns, the main novelty is the reinforcement of the bass by contrabassoon—the modern form of this instrument was not to be produced for six years (1879).[2] Generally, Brahms keeps the string and wind sections separate. For example, in the first statement of Variation III the winds have the theme and the strings act as accompaniment, while the roles are reversed in the repetition. This manner of orchestration contrasts directly with that in Wagner's *Tristan und Isolde* (see the excerpt earlier in the chapter). Interestingly enough, the scoring of the theme itself, so reminiscent of the eighteenth-century original, was not Brahms's first intention; he had placed the melodic line in the violins and violas.[3]

---

[2] McCorkle, NCS, 58–9.

[3] McCorkle has made some emendations, mostly involving addition of slurs, staccato signs, marks for dynamics, and clarification of accidentals, to the score as reproduced here; see his edition (in NCS), 149–58, for his comments.

BRAHMS: Variations on a Theme of Haydn for Orchestra (op. 56a)

Chorale St. Antoni

String Quintet No. 2 in G (op. 111)

Emphasis on chamber music for a variety of instrumental combinations is one of the hallmarks of the conservative stance Brahms maintained for most of his career. In the nineteenth century the genres of chamber music without piano, which previously had the greatest prestige, lost ground to those with piano. Yet Brahms continued to give equal emphasis to these more traditional genres, which included the string quartet and quintet and the less frequently encountered sextet.[1]

The Quintet 2, scored for the same instrumental combination used by Mozart[2] and Beethoven—string quartet with second viola—was composed in 1890 and published the following year. Brahms had intended this work to be his *opus ultimum*, at least with respect to the large forms of instrumental music, but his acquaintance with the clarinetist Richard Mühlfeld lead him to compose additional chamber music involving that instrument.

The Quintet is in four movements: an opening Allegro, an Adagio in *d*, an Allegretto in *g–G* and a Vivace in G. The main departure from the scheme standard in such a work is the third movement, where Brahms substituted, as he often did, a lyrical piece in moderate tempo for the usual scherzo or minuet. Because of their similarity to many of his character pieces for piano, such movements are frequently referred to as "intermezzos" (see "Late Piano Pieces, A," later in the chapter). The forms of individual movements correspond generally to what was traditional in this repertory. A sonata form with coda is found in the first movement and finale, although as in the finales of Brahms's symphonies 1 and 2 its development appears as a long episode in the recapitulation (b. 99 ff.). The second movement shows a free arrangement based on variation, but this form is implicit, not explicit. The theme is a group of contrasting elements organized like the exposition of a sonata structure but on a small scale. This is varied in what would correspond to variations II and III, both of which contain developmental passages; the last variation, IV, is shortened. The third movement is cast in the conventional three-part form.

In the first movement the Romantic emphasis on lyrical-melodic interpretation of the sonata structure is evident in the principal and the two secondary themes. The ascending third is prominent in all three themes and is singled out at the beginning of the development. Moreover, the third plays a prominent part in the themes of the second and third movements, providing an element of cyclic form, so often used by Brahms and others to achieve overall coherence. The development section of the first movement also contains extended passages of motivic development based on the principal theme (b. 69 ff. particularly), which accord well with yet another classical tradition.

Arnold Schoenberg once wrote that Brahms "repeated phrases, motives and other structural materials only in varied forms, if possible in the form of what I call *developing variation*," thus "showing consequences derived from the basic idea and

---

[1] The third movement of the Piano Quintet, *f* (op. 34), is in *NAWM*, and the first movement of the Clarinet Quintet, *b*, is in MSO.

[2] See MCP, No. 20.

remaining within the boundaries of human thinking and the demands of logic."[3] Everything in the composition, that is to say, is prepared by what has gone before. This may be observed in this Quintet. Note, for instance, in the first movement how the transition prepares the way for the first secondary theme, which in turn is varied to make the second secondary theme (see the cello part in the passage leading up to this, b. 34). Note also how the closing theme is based on a motive from the first part of the principal theme. This principal theme itself, for that matter, provides an example of the process in a fashion much like that employed by Haydn, as in the latter's String Quartet in C (op. 20 ii).[4] The second movement in particular is worth study under this aspect. Thus, although the developing variation is based on Haydn and other composers of that time, the radical fashion in which Brahms employed it, particularly the intellectual aspects, has made him seem, in this regard at least, something of a modernist.

The Quintet embodies the variety of expression and contrast that might be encountered in an eighteenth-century work. As is typical of Brahms, there are no literary or extramusical associations. The grandeur of the first movement's principal theme, forcefully initiated in the cello to tremolo accompaniment, is followed by folk-like lullabies in the secondary key area. Lyricism and tone color are combined in the passage in the development where a fragment of the secondary theme, transformed by augmentation, is exchanged between the violins in a hushed atmosphere over a tremolo in the lower instruments. The music of the central movements evokes the melancholy mood so often associated with Brahms. This contrasts with the pastoral quality of the midsection in the third movement, while the main theme of the finale is a Hungarian dance, a type frequently encountered in Brahms.

As with most of Brahms's large-scale instrumental compositions, this Quintet seems deliberately to invite comparison with great works of the past, aspects of which it adopts and reinterprets.[5] There is here a special affinity with Mozart's great Quintet, C (K. 515), clearly evident at the beginning. Brahms's preoccupation with genres of this kind testifies to his allegiance to the Classic tradition and thus to his aloofness in regard to the mainstream of musical composition at the time, represented as it was by the Neo-German group.

---

[3] "Criteria for Evaluation," *Style and Idea*, ed. L. Stein, trans. L. Black (New York: St. Martin's, 1975), 129–30; see W. Frisch, *Brahms and the Principle of Developing Variation* (Berkeley: University of California Press, 1984).

[4] See MCP, No. 9.

[5] See J. Burkholder, "Museum Pieces: The Historicist Mainstream in Music of the Last Hundred Years," *Journal of Musicology*, 2 (1983): 115 ff.

BRAHMS: Quintet No. 2 in G (op. 111)

Late Piano Pieces

A. Intermezzo, Andante teneramente in E (op. 116, no. 6)
B. Ballade, Allegro energico in g (op. 118, no. 3)

Apart from the song, Brahms emphasized the other small lyric form so prevalent in the Romantic period, the character piece for piano. He composed in this genre throughout his career, but with particular concentration during 1892–1893, when the two pieces printed here were written. For the most part Brahms avoided the extroverted virtuosic form fraught with literary associations, as in Liszt, preferring something more sober and reflective. Moreover, he rejected individualized descriptive titles and favored the more generalized intermezzo (his favorite), capriccio, ballade, rhapsody, and romance.[1]

While Brahms's structures here tend to be simple repetitive schemes, treated with some irregularities, elaboration may be found in the detailed accompaniment, with its intricate play of figuration patterns, counterpoint, rhythmic subtleties (especially hemiola), and chromatic harmonies. The expressive character of these pieces tends toward restrained melancholy, particularly in the intermezzos; the ballads and capriccios, however, are vigorous.

Brahms made a distinction in his character pieces similar to that of Chopin, between the larger form, the ballade or rhapsody, and the smaller, especially the intermezzo. The two pieces included here, both in three-part form, represent the two varieties. The first section of the shorter intermezzo is characterized by dense and rich chords (*dolce e ben legato*) that all but conceal the melodic line as it moves between the inner voice and the soprano. The midsection (b. 24 ff.) in g♯ is cast in the "aaba" form, with each phrase based on the same harmonic progression. Hemiola appears in both sections of the piece. The larger ballade is more forthright and direct. Again Brahms's density of texture is evident throughout as strong chords reinforce the melody. The well-defined structure features a midsection in B (the relative major) at b. 41 and a recapitulation at b. 72. A passage from the principal section appears in the midsection (b. 52 ff.), and a phrase from the midsection is used in the coda.

---

[1] AMA and CMS contain other intermezzi by Brahms.

BRAHMS: Intermezzo in E (op. 116, no. 6)

BRAHMS: Ballade in g (op. 118, no. 3)

Section Four: Bruckner

Allegro moderato (first movement) from Symphony No. 7 in E

Composed in 1881–1883 and published the following year, Bruckner's Symphony 7 received its first performance in 1884 under the direction of the well-known conductor Artur Nikisch. It is disposed, as are all his completed symphonies, in the conventional four-movement scheme, beginning with a broad first movement in the main key in sonata form and continuing with a deeply serious Adagio in c♯ [1] (Bruckner's memorial to Wagner, who died in 1883), a Scherzo in a with Trio in F, and a Finale once again in E. Bruckner scored the work for an orchestra of about the size found in Brahms's symphonies, differing only in the consistent employment of trombones, which Brahms ordinarily reserved for his finales. The enlargement of the orchestra in Bruckner's symphonic output commences with the introduction of a quintet of tubas in the second movement of this symphony.

The first movement clearly shows Bruckner's essentially lyric approach to sonata structure on a vast scale. The principal theme is a long, wide-ranging, through-composed melody—unusual for Bruckner in a movement of this sort—scored for cellos and violas. Its emergence out of the quiet tremolo in the violins is reminiscent of the opening of Beethoven's 9, which influenced him here and elsewhere. Following a scarcely identifiable transition, the secondary theme consists of commonplace, generalized elements, an ascending scale incorporating a turn, that in the late eighteenth and early nineteenth centuries would have been used to create thematic motives, but which Bruckner uses melodically. Thereafter, in the passage leading to the closing section of the exposition, the theme is presented in inversion (b. 103 ff.). Here this primarily contrapuntal device is divorced from its usual context and is used purely melodically. Elements of invertible counterpoint also appear elsewhere in this passage (b. 59 ff.). The concluding motive of the theme is then treated in an ascending sequence over a pedal point, building to a typically majestic Brucknerian crescendo—the model for which clearly was Beethoven. In the development (b. 165 ff.) all three themes are employed with principal and secondary themes in both regular and inverted forms. A new theme is contrapuntally combined with the closing theme at b. 221 ff. The powerful scoring of the principal theme dominates the impressive passage beginning at b. 233. The disguised recapitulation is almost unnoticed (b. 281 ff.) and is followed by the coda (b. 391 ff.). A great crescendo based on the second phrase of the principal theme over a tonic pedal point and another majestic celebration of the first phrase of the principal theme (b. 413) closes the movement with 40-odd bars of pure E.

The term feierlich ("with ceremony"), often used by Bruckner, provides a good characterization for much of his work. Styles associated with religious music play a key role here. One can point to the emphasis on counterpoint and related techniques

---

[1] Reprinted in S.

630

(notably inversion and imitation), the scoring, such as the organ-like quality of the woodwinds in the secondary theme, the "ceremonial" use of the brass choirs in the solemn chorale-like passages (development, b. 167 ff.; coda), the mighty fanfares prior to the closing theme, the restatement of the principal theme in the development (b. 233 ff.), and the coda. The source for this sort of expression is doubtless to be sought in Bruckner's long experience as student and organist at the monastery of St. Florian in rural Austria. In contrast to the religious influence is his interest in Austrian peasant dances, best exemplified in the scherzos and trios, but here suggested in the closing theme.

Bruckner has frequently been compared to Wagner, and in fact Wagner's music, which he admired, exerted a profound influence on him from the 1860s on. The two men were personally acquainted. Musically, we can point to the great length of Bruckner's symphonies, the magnificent effects of his large orchestrations, and the emphasis on sequential constructions, which could well have derived, in part at least, from Wagner. Moreover, there are direct quotations of Wagnerian themes, notably in the symphonies 3 and 8. On the other hand, unlike Wagner's music dramas, Bruckner's music shows little evidence of literary influence even though some of his works have extramusical associations. Further, the great length of many of the symphonies may result from his celebration of religious *maiestas* (majesty). Bruckner also remained conservative with respect to form, employing the traditional structural principles of the symphony. Thus, despite the association between the two, Bruckner's art clearly differs from that of Wagner in fundamental ways.

BRUCKNER: Symphony No. 7 in E, First Movement

Tempo I.*(molto animato)*

nach und nach etwas schneller

The Middle and Late Phases in Italy and France

Stylistic leadership in the fine-art music of Western Europe in the nineteenth century was in the hands of German, or at least German-speaking, composers, as it had been since the late eighteenth century. The situation is similar to that of the Netherlands musicians in the Renaissance and the Italians in the Baroque. German music now represented the mainstream, to which musicians in other countries had to react. Naturally the situation varied from country to country. Italian opera, for instance, continued to follow its own traditions, as in the past, relatively undisturbed by the evolution of music in the countries to the north. In France, on the other hand, we see a mixture of older traditions from the eighteenth century along with new types of opera unique to that country, where later in the century the influence of Wagner became strong.

Our examples of Italian opera come from the two most successful composers in the field at the time: Giuseppe Verdi (1813–1901), one of the most prominent figures in the history of opera, and Giacomo Puccini (1858–1924), his genial successor.

Section One: Italian Opera

Verdi: Selections from *Il trovatore*

    A. "Quale d'armi fragor," Scene, Aria, and Cabaletta, Act III

    B. Miserere Scene, Act IV

One of Verdi's most popular operas, *Il trovatore* is based on the Spanish play *El trovador* by A. García Gutiérrez and was first performed in 1853.[1] The plot involves two brothers, Manrico (the troubadour, tenor) and the Count of Luna (baritone), who have been separated since childhood and are unaware of their true relationship and who, moreover, are both in love with Leonora (soprano). Thus the dictum attributed to G. B. Shaw regarding Italian opera applies: The soprano and tenor want to make love but are prevented from doing so by the baritone. There are, of course, a number of complications. Their mother, the gypsy Azucena (mezzo-soprano), is important in the action and indeed may have been inspired by Fidès in Meyerbeer's *Le prophète* (see the excerpt in Chapter 2). The plot is difficult to follow because much of the action takes place between the acts. Verdi, who insisted on "subjects that are new, great, beautiful, varied, strong—really strong."[2] urged his librettist to preserve "all the novelty and bizarre quality of the Spanish drama."[3]

    Verdi composed in a fundamentally traditional way, with an orientation to the number opera (see p. 320), yet his treatment was varied and resourceful. While he generally respected the standard arrangement involving the aria and cabaletta, the large finale at the end of the penultimate act, the large concerted ensemble, and so on, he also alternated straight recitative with *parlante* and used a variety of aria types. Unlike Wagner, however, the emphasis was always placed on the vocal line, while the orchestra remained the accompaniment—the "giant mandolin," as it has been called. This is true of all his works, even though in the later operas the orchestra part became more elaborate and refined. Nor did Verdi employ Wagner's system based on the *leitmotiv*, although there are themes associated with characters and other aspects of the plot.

    Our examples show some of the range of affect encompassed here. In "Quale d'armi fragor" the end of Act III (No. 18 in the opera), Manrico and Leonora are preparing for their marriage in his castle, which is being besieged by the Count of Luna. Leonora is afraid, but Manrico assures her that their love will give them strength, and in his aria he vows to die in battle to protect her, if need be. Then Ruiz enters with the news that the Count has captured Azucena (the Count is unaware of her identity), whereupon Manrico orders his forces to arms for an attempt at rescue. The scene follows perfectly the standard organization of an operatic scene of the

---

[1] In the anthologies: excerpts from *Rigoletto* are in CSM and MSO, and from *La traviata* in MO and NSe.

[2] Verdi, *Letters*, ed. C. Osborne (London: Gollancz, 1971), 78.

[3] Ibid., 55.

period, as described earlier (see the discussion of Bellini in Chapter 2): recitative—aria—recitative (in which a new situation is introduced)—cabaletta. The only elaboration is the insertion of a brief duet with organ accompaniment. The scene may be outlined as follows:

Bar	Marking and Key	Type	Plot
1	Allegro assai vivo, c	Orchestra prelude	Uncertainty
9	Allegro, c (modulates)	Recitative	Manrico reassures Leonora
42	Adagio	Aria I, f–Ab (through-composed, first line repeated) II, Db (2 strophes with coda)	Manrico
83	Allegro, F	Duet	Manrico and Leonora, with organ
105	Più vivo, F–G	Recitative and *parlante*	Ruiz enters with news of Azucena's capture
138	Allegro, C	Cabaletta I (two statements separated by recitative)	Manrico musters his forces
225	Poco più vivo, C	II (coda: binary form with codetta)	Chorus joins in

Both the aria and cabaletta use rhythmic patterns and melodic sequence, as well as provide opportunities for vocal display, mostly in the cadenzas. Throughout, but particularly in the aria, duet, and cabaletta, phrases are regular (two or four bars) while the harmonies are clear and predominantly diatonic.

The other selection from *Il trovatore* is the famous Miserere Scene at the beginning of Act IV. Manrico has been captured by his rival and awaits execution in a tower. Outside, a choir of monks sings a funeral chant in the *falso bordone* style (homophonic liturgical choral recitative) as a bell tolls, while the agitated Leonora laments bitterly as she hears Manrico's song of farewell, with harp-like accompaniment, from the prison. The somber dotted-rhythmic pattern in Leonora's accompaniment was often used in the nineteenth century to symbolize death. These three elements are presented twice, followed by a coda (two parts with conclusion).

VERDI: *Il trovatore*, Act III, Scene, Aria, and Cabaletta, "Quale d'armi fragor"

A hall adjacent to the chapel in Castellor; a balcony at the back.

254

te - co   al - men   cor - ro a mo - rir! Al-l'ar -   mi! al - l'ar -
nev- er   for - sake,   nev- er for- sake.To arms   then! to arms

unis

te - co, o   te -   co a   mo - rir!   Al - l'ar - mi!   al -
die— by the fell   ty - rant's stake,   Com- mand us,   we

te - co, o   te -   co a   mo - rir!   Al - l'ar - mi!   al -
die— by the fell   ty - rant's stake,   Com- mand us,   we

259

mi! al-l'ar - - - - - - - - - - -   mi!
then! to arms! _____

l'ar-mi!   al - l'ar - mi! al-l'ar-mi! al-l'ar-mi! al-l'ar - -   mi!
fol- low,   to arms,   to arms,   to arms, to arms! _____

l'ar-mi!   al - l'ar - mi! al-l'ar-mi! al-l'ar-mi! al-l'ar - -   mi!
fol- low,   to arms,   to arms,   to arms, to arms! _____

263 (Exit Manrico in haste, followed by Ruiz and the Soldiers, amid a din of arms, the trumpet calling to battle.)

265

VERDI: *Il trovatore,* Act IV, "Miserere"

707

18
pal - pi - ti _ al _ cor!
is't _ death that is _ near?

Troubadour (from the tower)
Ah! _____ che la mor - te o - so -
Ah! _____ send thy beams, Au-

Harp

20
gno - - ra è _____ tar-da nel ve -
ro - - ra, Light _____ me to ear - ly

22
nir a chi de - si - a, a chi de-sia mo -
death, Waft her my long - ing, Waft her my lat - est

24
Leonora.
Oh! ciel!
Oh heav'n!

rir! ad-di - o, ad-dio, Leo-no - ra, ad-di -
breath! I leave _____ thee, Leo-no-ra, ah, I leave _

Verdi: *Otello,* Act III, Scene 2

Although Verdi had long shown an interest in the works of Shakespeare, as evidenced in his early opera *Macbeth* (1847) as well as in the extensive consideration of a projected *King Lear,* he became preoccupied with the great English dramatist in his late years. In collaboration with Arrigo Boito, himself a well-known writer and composer, Verdi produced *Otello* and 1887 and *Falstaff* in 1893.

Othello, Shakespeare's play of jealousy and revenge, provided good material for Verdi, as indeed it had earlier for Rossini. In the excerpt given here, Otello has been persuaded by Iago—whom Boito has converted into a diabolical villain—that Desdemona (Otello's wife) is having an affair with Cassio (one of his officers).[1] Cassio is in possession of her handkerchief, which has been planted there by Iago, who has stolen it. Desdemona, who suspects nothing and believes that Cassio is being wrongly treated, steadfastly denies Otello's accusations of infidelity.

Set as a continuous scene, as is characteristic of Verdi's late operas, this excerpt may be divided into several shorter sections. The emphasis is on recitative in its standard declamatory form, the *parlante,* and the lyrical arioso. Absent is the old set piece, the aria. Any sequence arranged in such a free fashion is naturally open to different interpretations. It appears, however, that from the "Lo stesso movimento" on (b. 70 ff.), the scene is set as a duet in a manner not different in principle from the duets Verdi had been composing since his early operas, so that the whole can be regarded as free recitative, with arioso and *parlante* passages, followed by a sectional duet. In an important departure from earlier practice (see Donizetti and Meyerbeer, Chapter 2), the expressive character of the music now corresponds to the dramatic situation. The scene may be outlined as follows:

Bar Number	Section and Form		Tempo and Key	Style	Plot	Remarks
1	I Recitative	A	Allegro moderato, E	Arioso	Otello and Desdemona exchange greetings	Recurring phrase; with ritornello; tonally closed
34		B	Allegro agitato, a (later c♯ and modulatory)	Parlante (also recitative)	Desdemona mentions Cassio; Otello asks about the handkerchief; Otello's narrative of the handkerchief, his warning against losing it, which Desdemona denies	Expressive figuration in violins, later violas
70	II Duet	A 1	Lo stesso movimento, G	Dramatic ensemble	Desdemona returns to subject of Cassio, punctuated by Otello's increasingly angry outbursts, until she breaks down	Note increasing intensity in Otello's part

[1] For Iago's famous "Credo," see MO, which also contains Desdemona's "Willow Song," along with the very end of the opera.

Bar Number	Section and Form	Tempo and Key	Style	Plot	Remarks
87	2	Più mosso, C	*Parlante* and recitative	The confrontation: Otello accuses her of infidelity, which she denies	
114	B	Andante mosso, *a* (later Poco più anima, then Come prima)	Recitative	Desdemona prays that Otello will recognize the truth of what she says; she weeps	"Death" rhythm at the beginning; later intense lyricism
150	C	Allegro agitato, *a*	Recitative	Otello rejects her; she persists in claiming innocence	
196	D	Tempo I, E	Arioso	Otello's ironical accusation	Recapitulation of the first section

(Otello sforza con un'inflessione del braccio, ma senza scomporsi, Desdemona ad escire. Poi ritorna verso il centro della scena nel massimo grado dell'abbattimento)
(Othello with a motion of his arm, but without changing his position pushes Desdemona out of the room. Then he returns to the centre of the stage in deep dejection)

Puccini: *La Bohème,* Act III conclusion

La Bohème was composed in 1896 to a libretto by Giuseppe Giacosa and Luigi Illica. Based on the novel *Scènes de la vie de Bohème,* by Henri Murger, which appeared in 1851, it portrays the life of a group of poor young artists and intellectuals living in Paris around 1830. The poet Rodolfo, the painter Marcello, the philosopher Colline, and the musician Schaunard are sharing an apartment in one of the poorer sections of the city. The main action involves the love between Rodolfo and Mimi, the consumptive seamstress, that grows from a chance encounter, leads to a falling-out and parting, and finally to a desperate reunion at Mimi's deathbed. Another love interest, between Marcello and the singer Musetta, provides contrast. Aspects of everyday life are shown in great detail: the suffering in the unheated apartment, the landlord demanding his rent, the merrymaking at the tavern, the street vendors, and so on. The great degree of realism and the concentration upon commonplace events associate this opera with the movement known as *verismo.*

In Act III, Mimi, who clearly is sick with tuberculosis, has come to tell Marcello of her troubles with the unreasonably jealous Rodolfo.[1] When Rodolfo unexpectedly enters, she hides and is able to overhear what he tells Marcello about his relationship with her, including his fear that she may soon die of her illness. Her presence, however, is betrayed by a fit of coughing, and as she enters, Rodolfo tries to make light of the situation. The excerpt begins as a farewell duet between Mimi and Rodolfo, which expands into a quartet when it is combined with a quarrel that erupts between Musetta and Marcello.

There are three sections, each consisting essentially of the same music, all in G♭, the first and last for Mimi and Rodolfo, the second including the bickering of Musetta and Marcello. The second has been expanded, the third shortened.

Bar Number	Marking	Type	Remarks
1	Andante con moto	Duet	Statement
28	——	Quartet (Two duets)	Expanded restatement
61	Più lento	Duet	Shortened restatement

Note the intermingling of musical styles: arioso, *parlante,* recitative, especially during the quartet, and the use of *violinata,* the doubling of vocal parts by instruments. Like Verdi, Puccini had a pronounced lyric gift and created many an eloquent and intensely expressive musical phrase—*motivo di prima intenzione.* This lyricism is much in evidence in this scene. Not only does the melodic line often shift from voice to voice, but also phrases introduced vocally subsequently appear in the orchestra (b. 3–5 = b. 30–33). Mimi and Rodolfo's duet includes reminiscences of the main love theme from Act I. The unison writing in their parts emphasizes lines important in the text. The descending dotted-triplet figure that represents the Bohemians in general is introduced at the conclusion (b. 68–70).

[1] Excerpts from Act I appear in MO and NSe (piano reductions).

PUCCINI: *La Bohème*, Act III, Conclusion

Section Two: France

French musical life around the middle of the century differed from that in the German-speaking countries. Instrumental music, particularly the large orchestral forms that had the greatest prestige in the Germanic Romantic tradition, was not well represented in the work of French composers. While Beethoven's symphonies had been performed in Paris in 1828 at the famous concerts conducted by Habeneck, most French composers, with the notable exception of Berlioz, did not take up the challenge and instrumental music did not become significant there until after 1860. Instead, opera received the most attention and Italian influence was strong. The French grand opera (see Meyerbeer, Chapter 2) maintained its supremacy until after the middle of the century, when it was supplanted by the *opéra comique* with spoken dialogue (see the discussion of Bizet later in the chapter). Toward the end of the century Wagner became a strong influence on French musical life, as attested to, for instance, by the operatic works of d'Indy. Finally, a distinctively French contribution lies in the repertory of symphonic organ music (see the discussion of Franck, which follows).

The examples in this section are taken from the works of César Franck (1822–1890), an organist who took a leading role in establishing instrumental music in the repertory of French composers; Georges Bizet (1838–1875), whose *Carmen* provides an early example of veristic opera; and Jules Massenet (1842–1912), the central figure in French opera at the end of the century.

Franck: Choral No. 2 in *b* for Organ (M. 39)[1]

Organ music, which in earlier historical periods had engaged the attention of the most important composers, declined markedly in the late eighteenth and nineteenth centuries. In the period 1750–1850 virtually no important composer made any significant contributions, save for Mendelssohn and Liszt. But after 1850 in France this changed: Large-scale pieces were composed for the gigantic organs of the French builder Aristide Cavaillé-Coll. These instruments sought to rival the symphony orchestra itself; hence the epithet, *symphonic organ music*, applied to this repertory.

Franck composed in a number of genres—chamber and piano music, orchestral music, particularly the symphonic poem, and church music—especially the oratorio—but he emphasized music for his own instrument, the organ.[2] His compositions for organ were freely-composed concert pieces. While generally a model for this sort of composition was provided by the large organ works of Bach, the example of German orchestral music was decisive, as is clear from the early *Grande pièce symphonique* (M. 29/op. 17) of the early 1860s and the later *Pièce héroïque* (M. 37) of 1878.

---

[1] "M" numbers are assigned to Franck's works in W. Mohr, *César Franck*, 2nd ed. (Tutzing: Schneider, 1969).

[2] The Sonata for violin and piano, A (M. 8) is in MSO.

Among Franck's last works are the three *Chorals* for organ of 1890, the second of which is reproduced here. In this work the relation to Bach is explicit, as Franck himself stated: "Before I die I am going to write some organ chorales just as Bach did, but with a different plan."[3] One difference here is that the chorales are not existing melodies (hymns), but were composed by the composer himself, as indeed had long been customary in French organ music. Still, the treatment remains indebted to the Germanic tradition, since Franck handles his chorale tune as if it were a cantus firmus in a fashion sanctioned by long practice. However, Franck adds a contrasting lyrical theme, which, after a grand rhetorical interlude in toccata style (Largamente con fantasia, b. 126 ff.), is combined with the cantus firmus during the fugue that concludes the piece. The work draws on the extensive coloristic possibilities of the organ. The many indications of registration are another particularly French preoccupation. Franck's harmonic resources are rich; they include extensive use of seventh and ninth chords, accented passing tones, tertian progressions, and extensive modulations, to E, g, eb, and f#, among others. The piece may be outlined as follows:

Bar Number	Marking and Key	Form	
1	Maestoso, b	Chorale statements:	1
			2
			3
			4
			5
65	Cantabile, b	Lyric theme:	a
			b
			a^1
			b
			a^2
126	Largamente con fantasia, b–g (chromatic)	Interlude	
147	1° Tempo ma un poco meno lento, g–eb–f#–b/B	Fugue on chorale and lyric themes, with passages in toccata style	

---

[3] Quoted by L. Davis, *César Franck and His Circle* (Boston: Houghton Mifflin, 1970), 244.

FRANCK: Choral No. 2 in *b* for Organ (M. 39)

Bizet: "L'amour est un oiseau rebelle" (*Habañera*) from *Carmen*, Act I

Bizet's most celebrated work was his last. Set to a libretto by Henri Meilhac and Ludovic Halévy and based on the novel by Prosper Mérimée, *Carmen* was composed in 1873–1874 and first performed in March 1875. The straightforward plot involves a conventional lover's triangle between Don José, the plain soldier, Carmen, the prostitute who seduces him, and Escamillo, the glamorous bullfighter who takes Carmen away from José. At the climax, the embittered José slays Carmen at the moment of Escamillo's triumph in the bullring.[1] *Carmen* was not a success at first, but it stirred up controversy by virtue of its lurid plot and detailed presentation of the lower-class milieu in which it is set. It thus may be regarded as a forerunner of the operatic movement that in Italy was known as *verismo* (see the discussion of *La Bohème*, earlier in this chapter).

Despite its serious and ultimately tragic plot, *Carmen* is an *opéra comique*, which makes use of spoken dialogue in place of the through-composed recitative characteristic of grand opera. However, *Carmen* is seldom heard in its original form, but rather in the version with the dialogue set in recitative after Bizet's death by his friend Guiraud for performances in Vienna in October 1875, where it scored an unqualified success.

An important feature of *Carmen* is the use of local color, particularly music inspired by the dances of Spain. A good example is the famous *Habañera* of Act I, the seductive dance by which Carmen entices José. Bizet believed he was adapting a traditional Spanish folk-dance melody here, but the tune had been composed earlier in the century by the popular composer Sebastian Iradier.[2] Set for solo voice with chorus, the *Habañera*, in common with folk dances generally, makes use of paired phrases. Specifically derived from Spanish music, particularly flamenco music, is the use of a minor key in fast tempo, the parlando-rubato quality with alternating triple and duple subdivision of the beat, and, of course, the pervasive *habañera* rhythm. All these are supported with a simple harmonic structure spiced with unresolved passing dissonances, mostly between the voice and the accompaniment. The aria has two strophes with refrain.

---

[1] The duet between Carmen and José in Act III is in MO; the end of the opera is in CSM (piano reductions).

[2] It is given by W. Dean, *Georges Bizet: His Life and Work* (London: Dent, 1965), 229.

BIZET: *Carmen*, Act I, "L'amour est un oiseau rebelle" (Habañera)

Massenet: *Manon,* Act II Conclusion

Massenet's *Manon,* composed in 1884 to a libretto by Meilhac and Gille, is based on the celebrated novel by Abbé Prévost, which was published in 1732. This novel had already served Halévy in 1830 (used for a ballet) and Auber in 1856 (adapted for opera, with a libretto by Scribe), and later it was to provide Puccini with material for the work that made his reputation. The action involves the unhappy love of Des Grieux, the sensitive son of a wealthy and aristocratic family, for the fickle, pleasure-loving Manon. Key roles also include Des Grieux's rival, de Brétigny, and Manon's older cousin, Lescaut. In common with many operas of the time, the milieu is that of the middle class.

Manon exemplifies a new type of romantic opera on a serious subject, which became popular in late nineteenth-century France. It differs from *opéra comique* in having composed recitatives instead of spoken dialogue. This type of opera is often referred to as *drame lyrique* or *drame musical.* The expression *opéra lyrique* (lyric opera) has also been employed.

Our excerpt contains the lovers' first parting, just before Des Grieux is to be abducted, under orders from his father, who desires to bring the liaison to an end. We can note the use of forms and styles long conventional in opera: recitative and aria, first for Manon, then for Des Grieux, and finally the concluding recitative when the abduction takes place, all preceded by a passage with spoken dialogue accompanied by music. Despite the fact that she knows of the planned abduction, Manon sings a song of farewell to the little table where she has shared meals with Des Grieux; then he sings of his hope for their future life in their own small home in the forest, the latter aria making use of the pastoral style. Massenet's sentimental lyricism is evident here.

The part writing is simple throughout the opera. The same applies to the basic harmonic structure, which is enlivened by such coloristic touches as triads with added sixths and other unresolved dissonances, along with occasional nonfunctional progressions. Three themes that recur throughout the opera are noted in the outline that follows:[1]

Bar Number	Style	Marking and Key	Text	Plot and Remarks
1	Spoken dialogue (with accompaniment)	Allegro moderato, G	"C'est l'heure du souper"	Des Grieux, having forgotten to mail the letter to his father, leaves to do so before dinner
16	Recitative	Allegro agitato, Eb	"Allons! il le faut!"	Manon, troubled, has feelings of unworthiness. Note expressive figure in orchestra
27	Arioso	Andante espressivo, Eb		
33	Recitative	Allegro, Eb		
38	Arioso	Très retenu, g		
42	Aria	Andante, g	"Adieu, notre petite table"	Manon's farewell to the table. Varied binary form

[1] Other excerpts are in MO (piano reduction).

Bar Number	Style	Marking and Key	Text	Plot and Remarks
65	Recitative	Allegro appassionato, C	"C'est lui!"	Des Grieux returns and tells Manon of his dream. Figure
76		Allegretto calme, A		from the first part of the excerpt. Love theme
97	Aria	Andante très calme, D	"En fermant les yeux"	Des Grieux's dream; pastoral style; through-composed
120	Recitative (also parlante, later duet)	Allegro agitato, c	"Quel qu'un?"	Des Grieux goes to answer the door and is abducted offstage. Recurring themes: from Andante expressivo in b. 120; Des Grieux's theme from earlier in the opera, b. 148.

TRANSLATION

SPOKEN:

Servant:
It's time for dinner, sir.

Des Grieux:
Yes, it is. And I've forgotten to mail the letter.

Manon:
Well, go mail it now.

Des Grieux:
Manon . . .

Manon:
What?

Des Grieux:
I love you! I adore you!
And you—do you love me?

Manon:
Yes, dearest, I love you.

Des Grieux:
Then you should promise me . . .

Manon:
What?

Des Grieux:
Nothing. I'll go mail the letter.

SUNG:

Manon:
Now! I must do it, for his sake.
My poor darling.
Oh! yes, it is he whom I love!
And yet I'm hesitant now.
No, no! I'm not worthy of him.
I hear that voice that draws me against my will:
"Manon! Manon! with your beauty you could be queen."
I'm all weakness and fragility!
Ah! in spite of myself I feel my tears running for those dreams that will be broken.
Can the future bring back the happiness of the beautiful days that have just passed?

Farewell, our little table
which so often brought us together,
farewell, farewell, our little table,
just large enough for the two of us—
it's hard to imagine—
sitting close together,
we had but one glass.
When we drank
we sought there the other's lips.
Ah! my poor dear, how he loved me!
Farewell, our little table, farewell.

Here he is.
I hope my pallor will not betray
me!

Des Grieux:
Finally, Manon, we are alone
together.
What? tears?

Manon:
No!

Des Grieux:
But it looks like your hand is
trembling . . .

Manon:
Here's our dinner!

Des Grieux:
Indeed! I'm being foolish.
But happiness is so fleeting and
heaven has made it so light that
one fears it will fly away!
Let's eat.
An enchanting moment, when all
fear has been driven away, where
we two dine together.
Yes, Manon, while walking I had a
dream.

Manon:
Well, who does not have dreams?

Des Grieux:
Closing my eyes . . .
Down below there, a humble re-
treat,
a cottage, all white,
in the depths of the forest.
Beneath its tranquil shadows
clear and sparkling brooks
reflected the foliage, sang with the
birds.

It was paradise. Oh! no!
that is all so sad and morose,
because it still lacked one thing,
you, Manon!

Manon:
It's just a dream, a foolish fancy!

Des Grieux:
No! that could be our life if you
wish it, o Manon.

(Knock at the door.)

Des Grieux:
Someone's here!
We mustn't disturb our party.
I'll send the intruder away and I'll
be right back.

Manon:
Adieu!

Des Grieux:
What's that?

Manon:
No, I don't want you to go!
You're not to open the door.
I want you to stay in my arms!

Des Grieux:
Child! let me go!

Manon:
No! No! I don't want to.

Des Grieux:
Let me go.
It's a stranger? how unusual!
I'll politely get him to go.
I'll be right back and we'll both
laugh at your foolishness.

(He goes out; sounds of a struggle.)

Manon:
My poor darling!

MASSENET: *Manon*, Act II, Conclusion

98

DES GRIEUX (à MANON avec intimité)

En fermant les yeux je vois.. Là bas... _____ une humble re-

100

-trai _____ te Une mai-son _ net _ te Tou _ te blanche au fond des

102 *dol.*

bois! _____ Sous ses tran-quil _ les om-

104

-bra _____ ges Les clairs et joy-eux ruis-seaux,

5

The National Schools

One of the most prominent features of late-nineteenth-century fine-art music is the incorporation of what are called "national styles." This involves the use of elements of vernacular, specifically folk, music from various countries. There was nothing really new about this. National styles had played an important role in the Middle Ages (notably French and Italian styles in the fourteenth century), the Renaissance (the Netherlands style, in opposition to the innovations in Italy), the Baroque (where the dominant Italian style interacted with traditions in France and Germany), and the Classic Period (thematic use of folk melodies by Haydn and Beethoven). In the nineteenth century, elements from vernacular music can be found in Schubert and Mendelssohn, and even more explicitly in Chopin and Liszt.

In the second half of the century the practice of integrating elements of vernacular music took on a different aspect, that of nationalism. In those countries that were not in the political, economic, or cultural forefront there developed movements directed toward the assertion of indigenous cultural values in specific opposition to those that were dominant. In the case of music, of course, it was the Germanic tradition that was preeminent. The earliest such nationalistic movement was in Bohemia, then part of the Hapsburg Empire. A similar movement developed in Scandinavia. But the most extensive and ultimately most influential such group was in Russia. The term *national school* is not applied to France, Italy, and England; and the schools in Hungary and Spain did not really form until the twentieth century.

Section One: Europe

Dvořák: "Dumka" (second movement) from Piano Quintet in A (B. 155/op. 81)[1]

The western parts of what is now Czechoslovakia—Bohemia and Moravia—had long had close ties to Germany. The region had also long been known for its music and musicians, especially in the late eighteenth century, and included such prominent and influential figures as the Benda brothers, Stamitz, Rosetti (Rösler), Mysliviček, and Vanhall. Early in the nineteenth century, two Bohemians in Vienna began working with what became the character piece (see the Schubert Impromptu, Chapter 1). Nationalistic sentiments began to make themselves evident in the 1830s and 1840s, first with the publication of folk-song collections, and became stronger in the aftermath of the revolutions of 1848 and the Austrian (Hapsburg) defeat in Italy in 1859. Planning for the Provisional National Theater in Prague, which was to give prominence to the work of native authors and musicians, began in 1862; it was to play an important part in advancing the careers of several composers.

The most prominent Bohemian composer of the time was Antonín Dvořák (1841–1904). In his attractive Quintet in A for piano and string quartet, composed in 1887 and published the following year, the slow movement bears the title "Dumka." This title refers to a type of Bohemian folk song, presumably derived from a Ukranian form. While the word itself means "to meditate, ponder or brood," as Howe says, it also "reflects the Slav temperament of emotional excitement, moving swiftly between the opposite poles of sadness and wistful longing on the one hand, and delirious activity on the other."[2] This contrast of affect is well demonstrated in this movement, which is organized according to the standard rondo scheme: a refrain (the melancholy part) with two contrasting episodes (joyful). Genuine folk melodies, however, are not used; as Dvořák explained in an interview during his sojourn in the U.S.: "I study certain melodies until I become thoroughly imbued with their characteristics and am enabled to make a musical picture in keeping with and partaking of those characteristics."[3]

Features found consistently throughout the piece include free treatments of binary form in each of the sections, a predominance of paired phrases, and the use of the same key ($f\sharp$/$F\sharp$)—only the first episode makes use of contrasting keys (D, G, g, and $B\flat$). Dvořák's melodic organization contains unusual reiterations of a single motive with variations. This also is characteristic of folk forms. Other folk elements found in

---

[1] "B" numbers assigned by J. Burghauser, *Antonín Dvořák: thematicky katalog* (Prague: Statni Nakladatelstvi, 1960).

[2] F. Howe, "[Dvořák:] The National and Folk Elements, "*Antonín Dvořák: His Achievement*, ed. V. Fischl (London: Lindsay Drummond, 1943/R Westport, Conn.: Greenwood, 1970), 250.

[3] Interview, *Chicago Tribune*, 13 August 1893, quoted by J. Clapham, *Dvořák* (London: David & Charles, 1979), 201.

the "dumka" proper (the refrain) include frequent melodic cadences to the dominant, the use of the lowered second, the raised sixth, and both forms of the seventh. Hemiola is prominent throughout. Note also the thematic transformation in the first episode, particularly the relation between its second section and its first, and that of the principal theme of the second episode. The movement abounds in counterpoint. Dvořák's use of folk elements in the traditional forms of Germanic instrumental music was typical of the national schools generally.

The following scheme shows the structure and other aspects of this movement:

Bar Number	Marking and Key	Structural Division[1]	Form
1	Andante con moto, f#	P	||o a a^1 a^2 o || ||: a^3 a^4 a^1 a^2 o :||
35		T	
41	Un pochettino piu mosso, D	1S	||b^1 b^2 c || ||: b^3 b^4 b^5 :||
84	Tempo I, f#	P	(Substantially as before, but different scoring)
119	Vivace (quasi l'istesso Tempo), F#	2S>P	Transformation of P^a; like a development in second part of the binary structure
178	Tempo I, f#	P	(Substantially as before)
213	Un pochettino più mosso, F#	1S	(Same as before, except for key)
256	Meno mosso. Tempo, I f#		(Substantially as before; scoring mostly recalls that of the first statement)
303	———	K	

[1] Symbols adapted from LaRue, *Guidelines for Style Analysis* (New York: Norton, 1979), 153 ff: in summary, P = principal or primary theme; T = transition theme; S = secondary theme; K = closing theme; 0 = introduction; > = derived from.

DVOŘÁK: Piano Quintet in A, *Dumka* (Second Movement)
(B. 155/op. 81)

Grieg: Selections from *Lyriske Stykker* (op. 47)

A. "Halling" (no. 4)

B. "Springdans" (no. 6)

In the first half of the nineteenth century, Scandinavian music was dominated by the German tradition as is evident in the work of Kuhlau, Gade, and Berwald. But the central musical figure in Scandinavia at the time, the Norwegian Edvard Grieg (1843–1907), proved able to develop his own style within an essentially Germanic orientation, drawing in elements of folk and traditional music.

Prominent in Grieg's works for piano is the series of *Lyriske Stykker* (*Lyric Pieces*), in 10 volumes (there are 66 pieces in all), composed between 1867 and 1901. These lyric miniatures, which are obviously modeled on Mendelssohn's *Lieder ohne Worte* (see the discussion in Chapter 1), contain a number of Norwegian dance forms. The examples in this chapter show two of the most characteristic of these, both from opus 47, composed in 1885–1887 and published in 1888. The "halling" is an acrobatic dance in duple time, and the "springdans," a leaping dance for couples. Both use the drone bass, an important element in European folk music generally. In the "halling" the drone remains fixed, as in a real folk dance, while in the "springdans" it appears at different pitches. We have already observed something similar in Chopin's mazurkas (discussed in Chapter 2). The "springdans," in particular, contains strong dissonances caused by the placing of dominant and other harmonies over a tonic drone, as well as by nonharmonic tones added to a triad, a practice reminiscent of Domenico Scarlatti.[1] This piece also features folk-like melodic organization by paired phrases, frequently with transposition. Like many dance forms, both pieces make use of different strains—in the "halling" three, with the first repeated at the end. But the "springdans" has a seven-part organization, with the first strain repeated in the midsection as well as at the end and then providing material for the short coda. The "springdans" also features alternation between units of four bars (first two strains) and six (second) as well as between duplets and triplets.

---

[1]See the "halling" "Hausgelat," from his *Slåtter* (op. 72) of 1902–1903, arranged from a dance for unaccompanied hardanger fiddle, on *History of Music in Sound*, ix, side 4, band 5. In this type of fiddle not only is a drone provided by unstopped strings, but the tone is enriched by the sounding of strings tuned in unison with those that are bowed (sympathetic vibration), all of which Grieg suggests in his arrangement for the piano. In the piece's midsection, however, the dance strain is submitted to a modern richly chromatic harmonization in a vein doubtless derived from Schumann. Grieg's own view of his relation to folk music may be found in *MWW*.

GRIEG: *Lyriske Stykker,* "Halling" (op. 47, no. 4)

GRIEG: *Lyriske Stykker*, "Springdans" (op. 47, no. 6)

Section Two: Russia

A central factor in Russian history since the reign of Peter the Great has been the adoption of Western culture, particularly that of France. *Westernization*, as it was called, of course affected music, with the result that up to the middle of the nineteenth century, musical life was largely in the hands of foreigners—Rutini, Hässler, Henselt, Jensen, and Field are among the most prominent. Opposition to this state of affairs and the important preoccupation with the achievement of an operatic style proper for Russian can be seen during the 1840s in the work of Glinka and Dargomyzhsky. After 1850 such nationalistic activity was centered in St. Petersburg around a group of composers known as *mogychaya kuchka* ("the mighty handful") or simply as "the Five." The group consisted of Balakirev, Borodin, Cui, Mussorgsky, and Rimsky-Korsakov, all of whom worked under the guidance of Stasov, the critic and writer.[1] Despite the large amount of polemic that attended their activities, their nationalism expressed itself in a fashion similar to other such schools elsewhere, with operas and symphonic poems based on Russian subjects and works of instrumental music that make use of folk song and dance.

This section examines examples from the most individual member of the Five, Modeste Mussorgsky (1839–1881), and then from the most celebrated Russian composer of the time, Peter Ilych Tchaikovsky (1840–1893), who was not associated with the group.

---

[1] See the excerpt in *MWW*.

Mussorgsky: Selections from *Boris Godunov*

A. Varlaam's song, Act I
B. Boris's monologue, "I Have Risen to the Highest Power," Act III

A biographical sketch that Mussorgsky prepared for Riemann's *Musik-Lexikon* (1882) includes a statement of his belief in what he called "artistic truth." Art in general— and music in particular—is seen, not as an end in itself, but as a means of communication; music and speech are viewed as interrelated, governed by the same laws and sharing the common goal of arousing human emotions. Instead of being preoccupied with beauty and external polish, the composer should strive for truth through the expression of genuine emotions in artworks directed at the broad mass of the people.[1] These ideas, based on Stasov, inform Mussorgsky's entire output as a composer. The artwork will be successful, as he wrote to Rimsky-Korsakov, if "the expression in sound of human thought and feeling *in simple speech* is truly produced . . . in *music* and this reproduction is musical and artistic."[2] This concept has found resonance from time to time in the history of music (compare, for instance, Monteverdi's notion of artistic truth as expressed in Book Five of his Madrigals in 1605).

Mussorgsky wrote his own libretto for his large and ambitious opera concerning the reign of the famous Tsar (reigned 1598–1605). The work was composed in 1868–1869, revised in 1871–1872 and performed in 1874. Although Boris is the central character, he by no means dominates the action. The Russian people in all their diversity are in fact the protagonists, and it is in this context that the extensive use of Russian folk melodies appears most appropriate. The scenes dealing with the Tsar portray in an extraordinary way his psychological disintegration. Having murdered the rightful heir to the throne, Boris is tormented by feelings of guilt, which are intensified to terror when a young monk, who, having learned of Boris's guilt, pretends to be the dead heir come back to life.

Our examples represent these two facets of this powerful work: the general Russian background and the psychological portrait of Boris.[3] Selection A, from the scene at the inn, is the vigorous ballad that the soldier Varlaam sings of the great victory won by Ivan the Great over the Tartars at Kazan. Mussorgsky follows the strophic form long associated with the ballad, but the accompaniment is varied from strophe to strophe in accordance with changes of mood. Each of the five strophes has five lines, which vary in the number of syllables. The first four lines form two pairs, while the last line is odd (i.e., "aabbc"). This ballad displays ambivalence with respect to tonality: "a" is in f (note the emphatic use of the Phrygian scale), "b" in a, while "c" cadences in G.

Selection B shows the tortured ruminations of Boris, who, having attained the summit of political power, is beset not only by unrest in the country and in his court, but by signs of impending divine retribution and the specter of his victim coming for revenge. No recognizable structural scheme is employed here by Mussorgsky. The

---

[1] Given in *The Mussorgsky Reader*, ed. J. Leyda and S. Bertensen (New York: Norton, 1947/R New York: Da Capo, 1970), 419–20.
[2] Ibid., 113. See also the excerpts in *MWW*.
[3] For the Coronation in Act I, see *CSM* and *MO*.

melodic style may be described as declamatory arioso, based on what had been developed by Dargomyzhsky, and there is some use of recurring melodic phrases, most prominently the one that first appears in b. 42. Note the suggestion of mental instability by the rushing chromatic figuration, a graphic instance of Mussorgsky's conception of artistic truth.

Until recently this opera has been performed in the version of Rimsky-Korsakov, who, among other things, altered keys and reversed the last two acts. Mussorgsky's original is more likely to be used today, as here (except that the piano reduction is given), so that the keys for the example given here may differ from those used by Rimsky-Korsakov.

TRANSLATIONS

A. VARLAAM'S SONG

Strophe 1

Listen to what happened at Kazan:
Tsar Ivan the Terrible sat in his
camp;
there he harried the Tartars,
so that they never again would
go on a spree in Russia.

Strope 2

At night he went right up to the
gates;
he had a tunnel dug under the river;
the tartars walked proudly around
on the city walls;
they looked scornfully down on
the Tsar,
fierce and full of cunning.

Strophe 3

Tsar Ivan grew grim and angry;
his dark eyes flashed wildly.
He called upon his cannoneers
to have their fuses at the ready,
at the ready.

Strophe 4

An impetuous young gunner came
up with a barrel of powder,
he put the tinder in the bung hole,
lit the fire, hey!
rolled the barrel along through the
tunnel;
what a bang that made!

Strophe 5

Hey! the Tartars were tossed into
the air
and with them the whole city!
And before the smoke had gone
away
there lay forty thousand Tartars
dead
and three more besides!

And so ends my warlike song!

B. BORIS'S MONOLOGUE

I have risen to the highest power.
For six years I have reigned in
peace,
yet there is no happiness in my
tortured heart.
In vain the fortune-tellers prophesy
a long and happy life and reign.
Yet nothing comforts me any more,
not fame, power, honor,
not the acclamation of the people.
At home I find no comfort:
I wanted to prepare a wedding feast
for my daughter,
my dear child, my pure dove:
but death stormed in like lightning
and took the groom away.

The hand of the Supreme Judge
rests heavy;
judgment has been passed upon my
soul;

around me all is in fearful darkness
and nowhere a ray of hope.
Woe is now deep in my heart;
my tired soul is full of fear and despair;
I feel a secret trembling . . . anxiety pursues me.
I had hoped through prayer to lessen the torments of my soul.
On the majestic throne, having accomplished everything,
I, Russia's ruler, pray for comfort, for gentle tears of consolation.

Conspiracies today, rebellion of the Boyars tomorrow,
here deceitful cunning in Lithuania, there secret plots;
hunger, disease and eternal destruction;

the people move like wild animals, the poor afflicted starving people! the poor country!
For all this misery visited upon us by God
in retribution for my bloody sin,
for all this the people hold me responsible:
I am the guilty one!

Sleep has left me . . .
in the darkness of night the bleeding child stands before me,
with flaming eyes it wrings its hands,
implores mercy,
but there was no mercy.
The wound gapes fearfully,
the death-cry harsh in my ear,
o merciful God.

MUSSORGSKY: *Boris Godunov*, Act I, Varlaam's song

MUSSORGSKY: *Boris Godunov*, Act II, Boris's monologue

Mussorgsky: Selections from *Pictures at an Exhibition*

A. "Promenade"
B. "Bydlo—Promenade"
C. "Ballet des poussins dans leurs coques"

In 1874 Stasov honored the memory of his friend and colleague Victor Hartmann, artist, architect, and designer, with a posthumous exhibit of his graphic work. Mussorgsky, who had also been close to Hartmann, was so impressed with the exhibit that he decided to commemorate it in his own way, by composing a cycle of character pieces, *Pictures at an Exhibition*. In a letter to Stasov he makes the inspirational nature of his approach clear: "sounds and thoughts hung in the air, and now I am gulping and overeating, I can hardly manage to scribble it down on paper."[1] Stasov arranged for the publication of Mussorgsky's work, providing descriptive material himself.[2]

The set consists of 10 character pieces, each associated with a picture by Hartmann. Continuity is provided by the "Promenade," which stands at the beginning and reappears four times, usually in varied form, between pieces of the set, thus effectively representing the viewer moving about the gallery. It is also reintroduced in two numbers at the end of the set. The organization of the entire work, which was doubtless inspired by Schumann's *Carnaval*, is as follows:

Mussorgsky's music	Hartmann's pictures (and remarks)
"Promenade"	
i "Gnomus"	A toy nutcracker in the shape of a gnome
"Promenade"	
ii "Il vecchio castello"	Watercolor of a medieval castle with a troubadour
"Promenade"	
iii "Tuileries. Dispute d'enfants après jeux"	Children playing and arguing in the Parisian park
iv "Bydlo"	Rough Polish ox-drawn cart
"Promenade"	
v "Ballet des poussins dans leurs coques"	Costume designs for a ballet: chicks in their shells
vi "Deux juifs, l'un riche et l'autre pauvre"	Two Jews, one rich, the other poor; also known as "Samuel Goldenberg and Schmuyle"
"Promenade"	
vii "Limoges. Le marche (La grande nouvelle)"	The marketplace of Limoges

[1] *The Mussorgsky Reader*, ed. J. Leyda and S. Bertensen (New York: Norton, 1947/R New York: Da Capo, 1970), 271.
[2] See A. Frankenstein, "Victor Hartmann and Modeste Mussorgsky," MQ 25 (1939): 268. Frankenstein's edition of *Pictures at an Exhibition* (New York: International Music Publishers, 1952) includes reproductions of Hartmann's artworks; more sumptuous is the edition by E. Lazarevna and V. Vladimirovicha (Moscow: Mezhdunarodnaya Kniga, 1975), which contains reproductions in color.

Mussorgsky's music	Hartmann's pictures (and remarks)
viii "Catacombae. Sepulcrum romanum. Con mortuis in lingua mortua"	The artist viewing the catacombs by the light of a lantern (the "Promenade" theme appears)
ix "La cabane sur des plattes de poule (Baba-Jaga)"	An ornamental clock representing the hut of the witch Baba Yaga, mounted on fowls' legs
x "La grande porte (dans le capitale de Kiev)"	The great gate at Kiev ("Promenade" theme appears at the end)

These pieces clearly show Mussorgsky's unique individual methods. The opening "Promenade," as he says, "nel modo russico" ("in the Russian style") is essentially through-composed, although it has some repetition of earlier materials, with irregular and changing meters (6/4 and 5/4, mostly the former), and tonal ambivalence ($B\flat$, with frequent cadences to F and g, the latter suggesting the Dorian). Subsequently the "Promenade" is varied, as between numbers iv and v (between numbers vi and vii, not included here, it is repeated in its original form). The other pieces in the set are mostly cast in the traditional three-part form. This is true of the selections reproduced here.

Graphic expressive touches are found everywhere in the set. A good example is the lumbering of the ox-drawn cart ("Bydlo"), with awkward dense chords in the bass; the melody, with its nonperiodic phrases; the strong suggestion (b. 1–8) of the Phrygian (orientation to $d\sharp$ rather than $g\sharp$, the tonic); the midsection, with its switch to B/b; its use of paired phrases (a prime characteristic of folk music, as has been pointed out) but with variation; and its hint at the melody of the "Promenade." Note the fragmentation of the melody in the diminuendo at the end, as the cart ostensibly passes into the distance. The cackling of the chicks in their shells ("Ballet des poussins dans leur coques") is evoked with chromatic figuration, mostly trills, in the high treble register,[3] and featuring nonfunctional alternation between F and the minor-seventh chord (dominant-seventh chord) on $D\flat$, but spelled with b natural instead of c flat.

---

[3] There is a small but venerable literature of this sort of expression; see Poglietti's *Capriccio über das Hennengeschrey* in A Treasury of Early Music, ed. C. Parrish (New York: Norton, 1958), 234 (No. 40).

MUSSORGSKY: *Pictures at an Exhibition, Promenade*

Bydlo—Promenade

Ballet des poussins dans leurs coques

Da Capo il Scherzino, senza Trio, e poi Coda

Tchaikovsky: Adagio lamentoso (fourth movement) from Symphony No. 6 in b (op. 74, *Pathétique*)

Tchaikovsky's symphonies stand in the central tradition of the genre—the large orchestral work with strong and clear extramusical associations in four movements in which certain conventional structures are used. Lyricism was crucial for Tchaikovsky: his works are carried by their expressive melodic themes, which at times reach an extraordinary level of intensity, always brilliantly scored. While folk materials appear in a number of his symphonies—and other works as well—his aim was expressive, not nationalistic.

A good example is his last symphony, composed in 1893, the finale of which is reproduced here. The work could well be described by the expression employed earlier in the century—characteristic symphony, a work whose expressive "meaning" is unequivocal and explicit.[1] The affect here is, as the title maintains, the *pathétique*, for which Tchaikovsky's choice of key is conventional enough. Yet this mood does not inform the work as a whole. While it is clear in the admixture of melancholy, consolation, and agitation found in the first movement and the somber quality in the midsection of the second, it is altogether absent from the boisterous Scherzo and March (third movement).

But there can be no doubt that the *pathétique* dominates the finale, a somber slow movement—an unusual way to end a symphony—where the feelings reach a pitch of desperation. The three-part form with coda is one common to slow movements. While the principal theme suggests melancholy (adagio lamentoso), the secondary theme (b. 30 ff.) in D, presented in two-part canon, suggests devotion (can lenezza e devozione), even though it contains the "sob" figure, conventional since the Baroque. This theme leads to a climax that suggests a catastrophic breakdown (abetted by the unexpected modulation to C). A second climax occurs during the restatement of the principal section, where the repeated material is replaced by an intense sequential and cumulating passage based on the first phrase of the theme (b. 108 ff.). This passage leads to a sustained climax over a pedal on E, and finally a restatement of the beginning of the principal theme, transformed, over another pedal, this time on F♯, leading to the true climax of the movement, where death is symbolized by the tam-tam (b. 137). This somber impression is confirmed by the passage for trombones and tuba that follows.

Note how the simple melodic line is distributed between the violins I and II and the woodwinds on the first statement of the principal theme. On the restatement (b. 90 ff.) the theme is presented simply and directly and thus with greater force. Throughout the movement the lower register is emphasized: the solo bassoon in the principal theme (b. 30 ff.) and again with horn on the restatement (b. 96 ff.), and particularly the coda, where the secondary theme is mournfully rehearsed in the strings (con sordini), then reduced at the end to violas and cellos.

---

[1] See his own account of his Symphony 4 in MWW.

TCHAIKOVSKY: Symphony No. 6 in *b* (*Pathètique*), Adagio lamentoso (Fourth Movement) (Op. 74)

115

155

6

The Late Phase in Germany and Austria

By the last two decades of the nineteenth century it had become clear that of the two central traditions, the Neo-Germanic and the conservative, the former had emerged triumphant. Brahms's sympathizers were in the minority, while Wagner's principles in one way or another were carried on by a number of prominent musicians, by no means restricted to the Germanic countries. The three composers represented in this chapter illustrate different aspects of the Neo-Germanic triumph: Hugo Wolf (1860–1903), in the *Lied*; Gustav Mahler (1860–1911), a noted conductor as well as composer, in symphonies and song cycles frequently of large proportions; and Richard Strauss (1864–1949), also a prominent conductor, first in the symphonic poem and later in opera (this last not represented in this book). Each of these composers had a strong literary bias. Wolf not only set poems by some of the greatest poets (Goethe, Michelangelo, Mörike), but also worked as a critic, while Mahler and Strauss composed music inspired by or expressive of either significant works of literature or great literary, philosophical, or religious themes.

Section One: Wolf

Songs

A. "Gesang Weylas"
B. "Prometheus"

What Chopin was to the piano, Wolf was to the German *Lied*. He composed in all about 300 songs, along with a small number of instrumental works and one opera (others were attempted). In these songs he took his point of departure from Schumann to the extent that he worked to establish an equivalence between the voice and the piano accompaniment. Even so, in his hands the accompaniment became much more important than in the past, while the vocal line was frequently cast in a declamatory style reminiscent of recitative. Consequently the old set forms play a less important role in Wolf: through-composition is dominant. His freedom of structure as well as richness of harmonic vocabulary may be derived, in part at least, from Wagner. Wolf emphasized Mörike, Eichendorff, and Goethe, whose poems he set with great sensitivity and often profound insight.[1]

The examples here consist of one small and one large song. "Gesang Weylas," composed in 1888, is set to a poem written around 1830 by Mörike, the text of which refers to a mythical island kingdom where Weyla is goddess, which figures in Mörike's novel *Maler Nolten* and elsewhere in his writings. The song is expressive of an exalted religious invocation. Its key, D♭, had been specifically associated by Beethoven with "maestoso," and here is reinforced by the marking "Langsam und feierlich" ("slowly and with ceremony"). The declamatory melodic line, the many repeated notes of which may relate either to liturgical recitative or to the oracular style of eighteenth-century opera (see the discussion of the finale from Weber's *Freischütz* in Chapter 1), the sonorous accompaniment of arpeggiated chords in chromatic harmony with telling tertian and other progressions, and frequent switches from major to minor all contribute to the atmosphere. The song is through-composed.

"Prometheus," composed early in 1889, is very different. Goethe's poem had already been set to music, notably by Schubert (discussed in Chapter 1) and as a matter of policy Wolf did not set a poem composed earlier by another composer unless he felt he could bring about an improvement. Although Schubert's setting is sufficiently long, ambitious, and intense—as is proper with this poem—Wolf's veritably explodes the bounds of the medium altogether. While Schubert had used B♭ (modulating to C), Wolf used *d*, the key long associated with the expression of the demonic, as in Mozart's *Don Giovanni* and Schubert's *Death and the Maiden* Quartet. The two settings have elements in common: through-composition (Wolf's contains some recapitulation), the use of figures with dotted rhythms (long associated with the

---

[1]The song "Anakreons Grab" is reprinted in CSM and MSO, and "Kennst du das Land?" in NAWM, both to poems by Goethe; three other songs are in AMA.

expression of grandeur and power), tremolo, octave doubling, and declamatory and arioso styles of recitative. But Wolf went further than Schubert. We can note the pronounced use of unresolved dissonances, the wide leaps in the voice part and accompaniment, and the explicit dynamic and other expressive marks in the score, which indicate the great degree of force that is at times required for proper performance. Melodically the oracular style of "Gesang Weylas" is also suggested.

As usual, Wolf provides an elaborate piano part, with an extensive prelude (which then serves as the accompaniment for the first part of the song, and elements of which are recalled later) and several interludes. Thus this setting is as ambitious as any in the nineteenth, or any other, century. This radical and extreme approach to the song is what most particularly allies Wolf to Wagner. The logical next step was to make use of orchestral accompaniment—and indeed Wolf actually did orchestrate some of his songs, among them the two reproduced here—but the symphonic song did not come into its own until somewhat later, with Mahler, Strauss, and others.

TRANSLATION*

WEYLA'S SONG

You are Orplid, my land,
shining from the distance.
From the ocean your sunlit shores
send up mists that moisten the
cheeks of the gods.

Ancient waters become young once
more
in your harbor, o child!
Gods, who are your servants,
kneel before your divinity.

*See pp. 56–57 for a translation of "Prometheus."

WOLF: "Gesang Weylas"

WOLF: "Prometheus"

Groß, kraftvoll und gemessen

Section Two: Mahler

Excerpts from Symphony No. 5 in c♯

A. Stürmisch bewegt. Mit grösster Vehemenz (second movement), a—Beginning
B. Adagietto (fourth movement), F, and Rondo-Finale (fifth movement), D—Beginning

Mahler's view of the symphony corresponded to that generally held in the nineteenth century; namely, that the symphony, which had become the central genre of musical composition, was, more than any other at the time, intended to be expressive of what was most significant and most grand. The ambitions of Berlioz have been mentioned, and Liszt's symphonies based on Dante and Goethe continued the trend. But Mahler went even further. "A symphony is the like the world," he wrote, "it must express everything."[1] Accordingly he encompassed in his 10 symphonies (the last of which he did not complete) an incredible range of ideas and emotions, from naive suggestions of natural sounds to the ultimate mysteries of death and resurrection.

What set Mahler apart, however, is not only the special nature of the emotions explored, but also the unbelievable intensity with which they are expressed. Along with the obvious folk-like elements (marches, dances, songs) one frequently encounters passages of great complexity and power expressing anxiety and distress, often heightened to desperation. The musical means for the latter sort of expression had been established by Wagner, notably in Act III of *Tristan und Isolde* (see the excerpt in Chapter 3) and Act I of *Götterdämmerung*. These are then juxtaposed with very serious lyric expression in some of the slow movements. Mahler's art reflects Wagner's treatment in its use of large orchestral forces (in several cases vocal forces as well), innovations in orchestration, and use of themes with clear associations or meanings, handled in a fashion derived from the Wagnerian *leitmotivs*. Mahler may be said to have brought Germanic Romantic music to its end and to have provided the point of departure for what was to come in the work of Schoenberg and his colleagues.

The Symphony 5, composed in 1901–1902 and first performed in 1904, belongs to his middle group of symphonies (along with 6 and 7), which not only lack vocal parts, but do not have descriptive notes to explain any sort of underlying program. Yet the musical styles used by Mahler have explicit associations, as in the earlier symphonies, so that the expressive content remains clear.[2] The symphony is scored for a large orchestra, involving triple and quadruple winds, six horns, and full percussion, including bass drum, cymbals, and tam-tam. It contains five movements, organized at the highest level into three parts, as in the symphonies 2 and 3 and as had already been done earlier by Berlioz:

---

[1] Letter to Sibelius (1907), quoted by C. Floros, *Gustav Mahler*, ii (Wiesbaden: Breitkopf & Härtel, 1977), 135.
[2] See, for instance, his own account of the Symphony 2 in MWW.

Part		Movement	Key
One	I	Funeral March	c#
	II	In stormy motion; with greatest vehemence	a
Two	III	Scherzo	D
Three	IV	Adagietto	F
	V	Rondo-Finale	D

Consistency of key, standard in the traditional symphony, is abandoned, here as elsewhere in Mahler, although one might be tempted to regard the first movement as an extended and complex statement of the leading note, since the rest of the symphony is not really unconventional with respect to key. This type of tonal organization is known as *progressive tonality*. At the same time, mood governs the choice of keys: *D* stands for affirmation and triumph, *a* for despair (see Mahler's Symphony 6), *c♯* for lamentation, F for lyricism. Portrayed in the symphony, then, is a progression of feelings not dissimilar to that of Beethoven's 5, one that represents the sequence *per aspera ad astra*, from the initial lamentation and outburst of despair to ultimate triumph, with a hymn-like passage in *D* near the end of the second movement suggesting the affirmative outcome.

The second movement (the beginning of which is excerpt A) must rank among the most intense and violent expressions in the entire literature of the symphony, unprecedented in its time. Note the strong gestures: the gruff and terse motive in the bass followed by the accented diminished-seventh chords, a gesture that can be regarded as an intensified form of the Baroque "sob" (first in b. 6–7), the raucous fanfare in the trumpets, the passionate—desperate—quality of the figuration in the violins, the rising accented chords in the trombones, and the suddenness with which it also seems to collapse at the end of the excerpt. The movement is a convincing aural image of a violent, desperate struggle against powerful and ruthless forces, which, in this section at least, prevail.

The last two movements, which together make up Part Three in Mahler's overall plan for the work, are to be played without pause. The famous Adagietto in *F*, with its light scoring (strings *à* 5, sometimes *à* 6, since the violas and cellos are variously divided, and harp), is a lyrical and sonorous piece in three-part form, thus (again using LaRue's symbols):

	P			S		P	
	a	a′	b		c	a	b
Bar:	1	10	23		38	73	87

It ranges from serenity at the beginning and end to a climax of great power in b. 95. The frequent exploitation of the highest register of the violins and the expressive *glissandi* impart a special kind of intensity. The midsection (S) has a disturbed and then passionate character. Note how the main melodic line wanders from one section of the orchestra to another (as in b. 9–10, from violins I to cellos and again, b. 16–17, to violins II). The rich chromatic harmonies, the dissonant chords, and the many changes of key all testify to the influence of Wagner. The midsection, for instance, moves from F to G♭ and then through E and D, suddenly back to the main key, F. In general the Adagietto is related to "Ich bin der Welt abhanden gekommen," one of Mahler's orchestral songs to poems by Rückert. In other respects the ancestry of this slow movement, which has counterparts in Mahler's symphonies 3 and 9, is to be sought in those powerful lyric expressions in the late quartets of Beethoven, the Cavatina in op. 130, the "Holy Song of Thanksgiving" in op. 132, and the Largo in op. 135.

In the finale, a long and complex rondo (the rondo element has two distinct parts) we find the exuberant tone full of reminiscences of folk dances (note the plodding drone bass) and bird calls, so common in Mahler. Particularly noteworthy is the transformation of the midsection of the Adagietto, which serves as the episode (as in the grazioso passages, such as b. 190). The movement also abounds in contrapuntal part-writing, as, for instance, in the second section of the principal theme (b. 23 ff.) and the passage leading to the episode (b. 166 ff.). At the climax of the movement, not reprinted here, the chorale-like theme from the second movement returns to bring the symphony to an optimistic and brilliant conclusion.

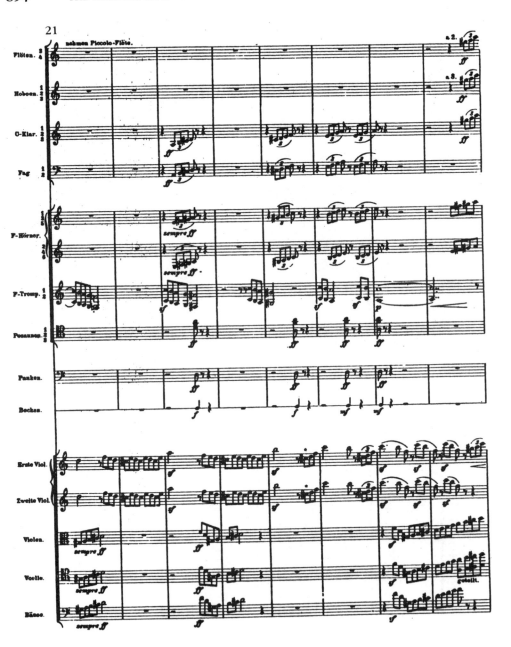

Fourth Movement

901

Fifth Movement, Beginning

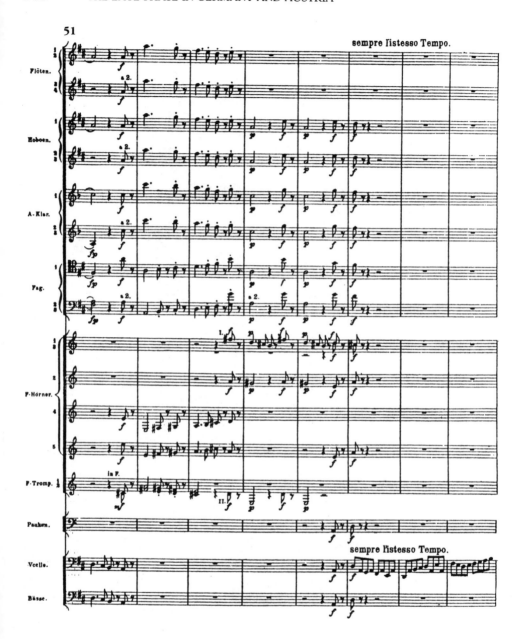

228

"In diesem Wetter, in diesem Braus," from *Kindertotenlieder* (no. 5)

Mahler, following Wolf as well as the earlier example of Berlioz, was the first to work in a consistent way with the orchestral song. Even so, some of his songs were composed with piano accompaniment, while others exist in both piano and orchestra versions. In his songs, Mahler rejected Wolf's emphasis on declamatory melody, through-composition, and elaborate accompaniment. Instead, he made lyrical melodicism the principal vehicle of expression, which was more in accordance with the Romantic tradition. But with respect to form Mahler was less conventional. In place of the older strophic and repetitive schemes, which, to be sure, find occasional use, he employed a free sort of variation that defies classification along conventional lines.[1]

The *Kindertotenlieder* (*Songs on the Death of Children*), composed between 1901 and 1904, show Mahler's dark preoccupations in a peculiarly poignant form. This orchestral song cycle makes use of poems by the Romantic poet Friedrich Rückert, written in the 1830s following the deaths of his son and daughter, Ernst and Luise, from scarlet fever. Mahler was apparently drawn to the subject by the memory of the early death of his younger brother, also named Ernst, and by fears for his own life after a harrowing illness in 1901. In a manuscript copy of the last song in the cycle, the one printed here, Mahler changed Rückert's "Mutterhaus" ("mother's house") to "Mutterschoss" ("mother's womb"); but subsequently he restored the original wording.[2] Ironically enough, Mahler's own daughter, Maria, was to die at the age of five, in 1907; yet at the time the *Kindertotenlieder* were composed he was not even married.

Kindertotenlieder consist of five songs, which explore various aspects of the peculiar sorrow and pain caused by the death of children: i, "Nun will die Sonn' so hell aufgeh'n" ("Now the sun once more rises so brightly"), d;[3] ii, "Nun seh' ich wohl, warum so dunkle Flammen" ("Now I really see, why the dark flames"), c; iii, "Wenn dein Mütterlein" ("When your little mother"), g; iv, "Oft denk' ich, sie sind nur ausgegangen" ("I often think, they have just gone out"); and, v, "In diesem Wetter, in diesem Braus" ("In this weather, in this raging storm"), d–D. The cycle is tonally closed. *Kindertotenlieder* mark a turning point in Mahler's song composition, away from folk elements and extravagance of gesture, to something more subdued and refined.

The example in this chapter, the last song of the cycle, is also the most forceful, as suggested by the way it is marked, "with restless, painful expression." While, strictly speaking, the strophic text is through-composed, a strophic plan is suggested by parallel melodic material in each section (strophe). Interludes occur between all but the first and second strophes. Two contrasting themes are prominent, one in the voice, the other in the accompaniment. The climax comes in the fourth strophe (b. 73 ff.), marked by ever-increasing intensity. In the fifth and last strophe agitation and passion give way to serenity. The key changes to *D*, and consonant, primarily

---

[1] Z. Roman, "Structure as a Factor in the Genesis of Mahler's Songs," MR 35 (1974): 157.
[2] E. F. Kravitt, "Mahler's Dirges for his Death: February 24, 1901," MQ 64 (1978): 329.
[3] Reprinted in *NAWM*.

diatonic harmonies enter along with elements of the pastoral style, notably bird calls, for the concluding *Wiegenlied* (cradle song), with the sweet sound of the celesta.

Note the graphic touches of instrumentation; for instance, the ostinato pattern at the beginning in the cellos and double basses in parallel thirds and with trills, later played *ponticello* and then given to other instruments, suggestive of a storm, as well as the combination of oboe and English horn for the main theme of the accompaniment, and the use of the celesta for the cradle song at the end. At the climax the use of the tam-tam is symbolic of death, here as in Tchaikovsky (see Chapter 5).

TRANSLATION

IN THIS WEATHER, IN THIS RAGING STORM

Strophe 1

In this weather, in this raging storm
I never should have sent the children out;
they should have been carried;
I had nothing to say about it.

Strophe 2

In this weather, in this strong rain
I should never have let the children out;
I was afraid they would get sick;
now such thoughts are in vain.

Strophe 3

In this weather, in this horror
I never should have let the children go out;

I saw to it that they would die tomorrow;
now that has been taken care of.

Strophe 4

In this weather, in this horror
I never should have sent the children out;
they should have been carried;
I had nothing to say about it.

Strophe 5

In this weather, in this raging storm
they are resting as if in their mother's house;
frightened by no storm, protected by God's hand,
they are resting as if in their mother's house.

MAHLER: *Kindertotenlieder*, "In diesem Wetter, in diesem Braus" (no. 5)

ich fürch-te - te, sie er - kranken;   das sind nun eit-le Ge

Allmählich langsamer

Section Three: Strauss

Prologue and Sections 1–4 from *Also sprach Zarathustra* (op. 30)

Strauss first attracted attention, even notoriety, and established his reputation with a series of symphonic poems. These are related to great works of literature, so that this old Romantic tradition retained its validity at the end of the century. The wide range of subjects explored in these symphonic works is matched by variety of treatment. In particular Strauss excelled at the portrayal of psychologically complex characters, such as Don Juan and Don Quixote and, in his operas, Salome and the *Marschallin* (in *Der Rosenkavalier*). As is typical with the symphonic poem, form grows out of the subject matter. While some are free, unrelated to any preconceived scheme, others employ traditional forms such as the rondo (*Till Eulenspiegel* [op. 28]) or theme and variations (*Don Quixote* [op. 35]).[1] For the most part Strauss's treatment is both extroverted and extravagant, as he calls upon the full resources of harmony and orchestration in the Wagnerian mold.

The work selected here, *Also sprach Zarathustra* (*Thus Spake Zarathustra*), composed in 1895–1896, represents the first of Strauss's larger symphonic poems. Although it is based on Nietzsche's philosophical work of the same title, written in 1883–1891, Strauss's work was not intended musically to realize Nietzsche's concepts, even though the subtitle states "freely after Nietzsche." He explained in a letter:

> I did not intend to write philosophical music, or portray Nietzsche's great work musically. I meant rather to convey in music an idea of the evolution of the human race from its origin through the various phases of development, religious as well as scientific, up to Nietzsche's idea of the *Übermensch* [*Superman*]. The whole symphonic poem is intended as my homage to Nietzsche's genius, which found its greatest exemplification in his book, *Also sprach Zarathustra*.[2]

Strauss also described the work as "symphonic optimism in fin-de-siècle form, dedicated to the twentieth century."[3]

The traditional interpretation of *Also sprach Zarathustra* involves the struggle of man (Zarathustra) to solve the riddle of nature and life itself. After the glory of the sunrise (Prologue), a celebration of nature, different aspects of human activity and evolution are explored (organized religion, joys and passions, mourning, science). After a crisis and convalescence, a dance grows to an orgy and then subsides as the

---

[1] *Till Eulenspiegel* is reprinted in MSO, an excerpt from *Don Quixote* appears in NAWM, and an excerpt from the opera *Salome* is in MO.

[2] Quoted by N. Del Mar, *Richard Strauss: A Critical Commentary on his Life and Work*, i (London: Barrie & Rockcliff, 1962), 134.

[3] Quoted by W. Schuh, *Richard Strauss: A Chronicle of the Early Years, 1864–1898*, trans. M. Whittall (Cambridge, England: Cambridge University Press, 1982), 418.

clock strikes 12:00. Following the serene Epilogue the piece ends ambiguously, as if the riddle has not been solved.

The composition features three cyclic themes, which Strauss treats like Wagnerian *leitmotivs*: (1) the "Nature" or "Sunrise" theme, consisting of the most basic of musical intervals, the octave and fifth; (2) a rising triadic theme associated with the "Inquiring spirit," constantly and restlessly striving to comprehend nature; and (3) the "Satiety" theme, a chromatic fanfare depicting Man's reaction against excess. All three appear in the excerpt reproduced here. Strauss also employs key symbolism: C stands for Nature, B for Man and his striving. This dualism is made explicit at the end, where the two are juxtaposed.

EXAMPLE 3.   LEITMOTIVS IN STRAUSS' *ALSO SPRACH ZARATHUSTRA*

Nature/Sunrise

The Inquiring Spirit

Saiety

This conventional view of the work, however, does not accord well with Strauss's stated intentions, as quoted earlier: It particularly does not address the *Übermensch*. A new interpretation has been advanced by Peter Franklin,[4] in which the central aspect of the work is not the quest for the truth behind nature and existence; rather, Zarathustra is viewed as the central figure in a narrative, who undertakes a journey of "self-discovery towards the literal 'self-overcoming' that is ultimately to produce the Nietzschean *Übermensch*."[5] This "self-overcoming" takes place during the intoxicating dance and subsequent "Night-wanderer's Song," the true climax of the work. Here the conventional limits imposed by society are overcome, not through reason, but through dance and drunkenness, which reveal the experience of life in all its profundity. In this interpretation, the first of the themes cited previously stands not just for the sunrise but for the Will in Schopenhauer's sense, the basic driving force of the universe. By

[4] P. Franklin, "Strauss and Nietzsche: A Revaluation of 'Zarathustra,'" MR, 32 (1971): 249.
[5] Ibid., 250.

penetrating to the center of life and overcoming the Will, Man can reach the stage of the *Übermensch*. The ambiguous ending symbolizes Nietzsche's idea of eternal recurrence: The piece could begin all over again.

Thus Zarathustra's progress in confronting and overcoming the Will involves (see the chart that follows) encounters with Christianity (note the quotations from Gregorian chant), which, though appealing, is found wanting (i and ii), the emotions (joys, passions, sorrow [iii and iv]), then science (v), at which point the crisis occurs, symbolized by a crescendo and a grand restatement of the Sunrise (Will) theme. The convalescent Zarathustra is then awakened (vi), and proceeds to find fulfillment in dance and intoxication (vii and viii). The Satiety theme first appears, suitably enough, at the end of iii, and plays an increasingly important role, particularly in the final portions of the work, where it is transformed so as to evoke a feeling of resigned and peaceful acceptance.

Also sprach Zarathustra is in a free form containing eight more or less clearly defined sections that correspond to parts of Nietzsche's book, although Strauss has rearranged their order. The last section, "Das Nachtwandlerlied" is not taken directly from Nietzsche, but it corresponds to his *"Das trunkene Lied"* ("The Drunken Song"), as the context and the bell striking 12:00 make clear. Herewith the outline of the entire work:

Section	Title	Remarks
	Zarathustra's Prologue	The sunrise
i	Von den Hinterweltlern (Of the Metaphysicians; literally, "those that live behind the world")[1]	Orthodox religion; the organ quotes a Gregorian chant melody for Credo
ii	Von der grossen Sehnsucht (Of the Great Yearning)	The organ quotes a Gregorian chant melody for Magnificat
iii	Von den Freuden und Leidenschaften (Of Joys and Passions)	Intensely passionate, loud and forceful
iv	Das Grablied (Song of the Grave)	Mournful
v	Von der Wissenschaft (Of Science)	Fugue on a chromatic subject containing all 12 tones
vi	Der Genesende (The Convalescent)	Double fugue, then bright fanfares, leading to grand climax
vii	Das Tanzlied (The Dance Song)	Trivial Viennese waltz
viii	Das Nachtwandlerlied (Song of the Night Wanderer)[2]	The bell tolls 12:00
	Epilogue	Harmonic ambiguity at end, B versus C

[1] See the annotated translation of Nietzsche's *Also sprach Zarathustra* by W. Kaufmann (New York: Viking, 1966), 5. In Strauss's original version the section was called "Vom Göttlichen" ("Of the Godlike"), a heading, interestingly enough, not found in Nietzsche, but that corresponds to the character of the music; see Del Mar, *Richard Strauss*, i, 136.

[2] The first edition of the score has *Das Nachwandlerlied* (*Song of Him Who Wanders Afterwards*), probably a misprint.

Strauss calls for a large orchestra, one that includes the bass drum, cymbals, harps, glockenspiel, and organ, along with six horns, two bass tubas, the usual woodwinds, but including contrabassoon, and a large complement of strings. The opening is famous: the organ, the trumpet signal (Nature or the Will), the accented chords in *molldur*, and the timpani, all in a grandiose portrayal of the sunrise. The section "Von den Hinterweltlern" has extensive *divisi* writing for the strings, carried out to 16 parts, to make an extraordinary effect. Throughout, the solo and coloristic use of woodwinds and brass is prominent. Extensive use of counterpoint combines with the chromatically charged harmonies, changing of keys, and skillful orchestration to produce a powerful effect.

Our excerpt consists of the Prologue and the first four sections.

STRAUSS: *Also sprach Zarathustra*, Prologue and Sections 1-4 (op. 30)

*) Die Orgel sehr schwach zu registrieren, so dass sie durchgängig als begleitend und die Streichinstrumente als führend erscheinen.

67

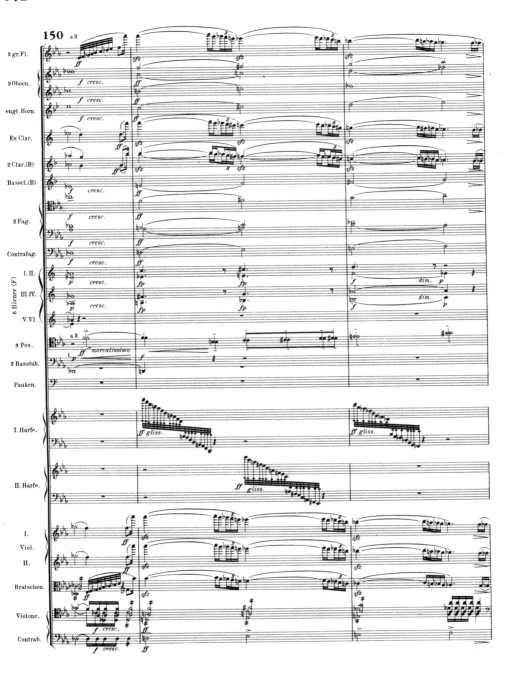

Appendix A: List of Editions*

BELLINI
Norma (Reale accademia d'Italia, v; Rome, 1935)

BERLIOZ
a. *Werke.* Ed. C. Malherbe and F. Weingartner. 18 vols. (Leipzig: Breitkopf & Härtel, 1900–1907/R 25 vols. New York: Kalmus, n.d.)
b. *New Edition of the Complete Works* (Kassel: Bärenreiter, since 1967)

BIZET
Carmen. Ed. F. Oeser (Kassel: Bärenreiter, 1964); this ed. changes the stage directions and omits Bizet's last revisions

BRAHMS
Sämtliche Werke. Ausgabe der Gesellschaft der Musikfreunde in Wien. 26 vols. (Leipzig: Breitkopf & Härtel, 1926–1927/R Wiesbaden & New York, 1971)

BRUCKNER
Sämtliche Werke. Ed. L. Nowak (Vienna: Musikwissenschaftlicher Verlag, since 1953)

CHOPIN
Henle eds. of piano music, available separately. Ed. E. Zimmermann (Munich: Henle, since 1956)

DONIZETTI
Collected Works (London: Egret House, since 1973)

DVOŘÁK
Souborné vydání. Ed. O. Sourek (Prague: Artia, since 1955)

FRANCK
Oeuvres complètes pour orgue. Édition originale. 4 vols. (Paris: Durand, n.d.)

GRIEG
Gesamtausgabe (Frankfurt & New York: Peters, since 1977)

LISZT
a. *Musikalische Werke.* Herausgegeben von der Liszt-Stiftung. 32 vols. (Leipzig: Breitkopf & Härtel, 1908–1933/R Farnsborough: Gregg, 1966, and New York: Kalmus, n.d.)
b. *Neue Ausgabe sämtlicher Werke* (Budapest: Editio Musica, since 1970)

MAHLER
Sämtliche Werke (Vienna: Universal, since 1960)

MENDELSSOHN
a. *Werke.* Ed. J. Rietz. 36 vols. (Leipzig: Breitkopf & Härtel, 1874–1877/R Farnsborough: Gregg, 1967–1968)
b. *Leipziger Ausgabe der Werke* (Leipzig: Deutscher Verlag für Musik, since 1960)

MUSSORGSKY
Sämtliche Werke. Ed. P. Lamm. 21 vols. (Moscow: Stadtmusikverlag, 1928–1934/R 98 vols., New York: Kalmus, 1969)

SCHUBERT
a. *Werke.* Kritische durchgesehene Gesamtausgabe. 41 vols. & 3 supplements (Leipzig: Breitkopf & Härtel, 1884–1897/R New York: Dover, 1965, and Huntington: Kalmus, 1971)
b. *Neue Ausgabe sämtlicher Werke* (Kassel: Bärenreiter, since 1964).

SCHUMANN
Werke. Ed. C. Schumann. 34 vols. (Leipzig: Breitkopf & Härtel, 1881–1893/R Farnsborough: Gregg, 1967–1968)

TCHAIKOVSKY
Complete Works (Moscow: Mezhdunarodnaya Kniga, since 1940)

VERDI
Critical Edition of Works. Ed. P. Gossett

---

*Note: Only historical–critical editions are shown. The works of some of the composers included in this volume have yet to be edited in this fashion.

(Chicago: University of Chicago Press, since 1983)

WAGNER

   a. *Werke.* Ed. M. Balling. 10 vols. (incomplete) (Leipzig, Breitkopf & Härtel, 1912–1929/R New York: Dover, 1971)

   b. *Sämtliche Werke.* Ed. C. Dahlhaus (Mainz: Schott, since 1970)

WOLF

   Sämtliche Werke. Kritische Gesamtausgabe. Ed. H. Jancik (Vienna: Musikwissenschaftlicher Verlag, since 1960)

Appendix B: Secondary Literature

This bibliography is limited to books in English. It emphasizes those that provide balanced and up-to-date accounts of their subjects, giving preference to those that take up music over those that are purely biographical; occasionally older books are listed. In most cases only one book is shown for each composer. There is nothing really suitable for Meyerbeer. See also the notes to the commentaries as well as the list in Abbreviations for Publications Frequently Cited.

BACKGROUND

General

M. Abrams, *The Mirror and the Lamp* (New York: Oxford, 1953)

L. Furst, *Romanticism in Perspective*, 2nd ed. (London: Macmillan, 1979)

H. Jones, *Revolution and Romanticism* (Cambridge, Mass.: Belknap Press of Harvard University Press, 1974)

Music

G. Abraham, *A Hundred Years of Music* (London: Duckworth, 1938/R Chicago: Aldine, 1964)

The Age of Beethoven, ed. G. Abraham (*New Oxford History of Music*, viii; London: Oxford, 1982)

A. Einstein, *Music in the Romantic Era* (New York: Norton, 1947)

D. Grout, *A Short History of Opera*, 2nd ed. (New York: Columbia, 1965)

F. Kirby, *A Short History of Keyboard Music* (New York: Schirmer, 1966)

R. Longyear, *Nineteenth-century Romanticism in Music*, 2nd ed. (Englewood Cliffs, N.J.: Prentice-Hall, 1973)

L. Plantinga, *Romantic Music* and *Anthology of Romantic Music*, 2 vols. (New York: Norton, 1984)

D. Tovey, *Essays in Musical Analysis*, 6 vols. (London: Oxford, 1935–1939/R with some omissions, 2 vols., 1981)

INDIVIDUAL COMPOSERS

Bellini

H. Weinstock, *Vincenzo Bellini: His Life and His Operas* (New York: Knopf, 1971)

Berlioz

H. Macdonald, *Berlioz* (London: Dent, 1982)

Bizet

W. Dean, *Georges Bizet, His Life and Work* (London: Dent, 1965)

Brahms

K. Geiringer, *Brahms, His Life and Work*, 3rd ed. (New York: Da Capo, 1981)

Bruckner

D. Watson, *Bruckner* (London: Dent, 1975)

Chopin

A. Walker (ed.), *Frederic Chopin: Profiles of the Man and Musician* (London: Barrie & Rockcliff, 1966)

Donizetti

W. Ashbrook, *Donizetti and His Operas* (Cambridge, England: Cambridge University Press, 1982)

Dvořák

J. Clapham, *Dvořák* (London: David & Charles, 1979)

Franck

L. Davis, *César Franck and His Circle* (Boston: Houghton Mifflin, 1970)

Grieg

G. Abraham (ed.), *Grieg: A Symposium* (London: Lindsay Drummond, 1948/R Norman: University of Oklahoma Press, 1950).

Liszt

A. Walker (ed.), *Franz Liszt, The Man and His Music* (New York: Taplinger, 1970)

A. Walker, *Franz Liszt: The Virtuoso Years, 1811–47* (New York: Knopf, 1983)

Mahler

E. Gartenberg, *Mahler, The Man and His Music* (N. Y.: Schirmer, 1978)

D. Mitchell, *Gustav Mahler*, 2 vols.: i, *The Early Years*, ed. P. Banks & D. Matthews (Berkeley & Los Angeles, University of California Press, 1980; orig. ed., 1958); ii, *The Wunderhorn Years* (Boulder: Westview, 1975)

Massenet

J. Harding, *Massenet* (New York: St. Martin's, 1970)

Mendelssohn

E. Werner, *Mendelssohn: A New Image of the Composer and His Age* (New York: Free Press, 1963)

Mussorgsky

M. Brown (ed.), *Mussorgsky In Memoriam, 1881–1981* (Ann Arbor: UMI, 1982)

A. Orlova, *Mussorgsky's Days and Works. A Biography in Documents*, trans. R. Guenther (Ann Arbor: UMI, 1983)

Puccini

C. Osborne, *The Complete Operas of Puccini* (London: Gollancz, 1981)

Schubert

A. Einstein, *Schubert, A Musical Portrait* (New York & Oxford: Oxford University Press, 1952/R 1981)

Schumann

G. Abraham (ed.), *Schumann: A Symposium* (Cambridge, England: Cambridge University Press, 1952)

A. Walker (ed.), *Schumann. The Man and His Music* (London: Barrie & Jenkins, 1972)

Strauss

N. Del Mar, *Richard Strauss: A Critical Commentary on His Life and Work*, 3 vols. (London: Barrie & Rockcliff; Philadelphia: Chilton, 1962–1972)

Tchaikovsky

E. Garden, *Tchaikovsky* (London: Dent, 1973)

Verdi

J. Budden, *The Operas of Verdi*, 3 vols.: i, *From Oberto to Rigoletto* (New York: Praeger, 1973); ii, *From Il trovatore to La Forza del destino* (London: Cassell, 1978); iii, *From Don Carlo to Falstaff* (New York: Oxford, 1981)

Wagner

P. Burbridge & R. Sutton (eds.), *The Wagner Companion* (London: Faber & Faber, 1979)

E. Newman, *The Wagner Operas* (New York: Knopf, 1972; orig. ed., 1949)

Weber

J. Warrack, *Carl Maria von Weber* (New York: Macmillan, 1968)

Wolf

E. Sams, *The Songs of Hugo Wolf* (London & New York: Oxford, 1961; 2nd ed., 1981/R 1983)